John,

Best wishes &
good hunting.

Gratten
2004

Turkey Dog Tales

By

Gratten Hepler

Gratten Hepler

1663 LIBERTY DRIVE, SUITE 200
BLOOMINGTON, INDIANA 47403
(800) 839-8640
WWW.AUTHORHOUSE.COM

© 2004 Gratten Hepler.
All Rights Reserved.

No part of this book may be reproduced, stored in a retrieval system, or transmitted by any means without the written permission of the author.

First published by AuthorHouse 10/20/04

ISBN: 1-4184-8326-5 (sc)

Printed in the United States of America
Bloomington, Indiana

This book is printed on acid-free paper.

ACKNOWLEDGMENTS

Many of the accomplishments in our lives wouldn't have been possible had it not been for the help of other people, either directly or indirectly. This is certainly true in the writing of this book.

First and foremost, I would like to thank my wonderful wife, Valerie. Without her encouragement along the way, I wouldn't have been able to complete this project. No one knows my passion for turkey hunting better than Valerie. She has never objected to the time I have spent turkey hunting. She has also helped me with my turkey dogs over the years in many ways. Valerie has made excellent table fare out of many of the turkeys I've brought home. Her tremendous help in editing this book, spending countless hours on this task, is greatly appreciated. I dare say that without a loving and supportive wife like Valerie, my turkey hunting experience would have been greatly diminished.

My two sons, Bert and Ben, have also been instrumental in this book. Without their initial encouragement and support, this book would have never been possible. There are also stories of turkey hunting with both Bert and Ben contained in this book.

Even though my mom and dad are no longer with us, I owe them many thanks. My dad was responsible for introducing me to turkey hunting at a very young age. Both my mom and dad gave me support numerous times when I came home after an unproductive hunt. They also consoled me after many misses I experienced during my early years turkey hunting.

I would like to thank my good friend, John Stone, and his dad, Med Stone, who introduced me to hunting turkeys with a dog. John and Med also offered valuable advice for training my first turkey dog.

Lastly, I would like to thank all the good friends who have hunted with me through the years and helped provide some of the many fine memories that I could write about

FOREWORD

There are two distinctly different forms of turkey hunting: spring turkey season and fall turkey season. During the spring season, the hunter goes afield and listens for gobbling toms in search of a mate. If the spring hunter is lucky, he can position himself in such a way that the gobbler will come close enough to the hunter's calling that the hunter will have a shot. The hunter must call convincingly because most of the time in nature, the hen will go to the gobbling tom. While I am a devoted spring gobbler hunter, this book is dedicated to the fall season.

Turkeys in the fall of the year normally flock together in family groups. The fall hunter will primarily be hunting these family flocks—the old hen and her young of that year. The young gobblers are called jakes, and the young hens are called jennies. If luck is on the hunter's side, he may run into a flock of old gobblers.

The fall hunter has several options as to how he wants to hunt the wild turkey. Some of these options include stalking, still hunting, lying in ambush in a blind, or trying to call in a lone bird or possibly a whole flock. The most exciting method, in my opinion, is to find a flock of turkeys, flush and scatter them, and then attempt to call the birds back.

Once a flock of turkeys is scattered, their instinct drives them to try to regroup with other members of their flock. Finding a gang of birds in the fall can be a very difficult task. The turkeys can range over a very large area, especially if food is scarce.

Having a good turkey dog can help tremendously in locating a flock. Dogs can use their great sense of smell in trailing, or winding, the birds at great distances. Good turkey dogs can also use their other senses of hearing and sight to help find the turkeys. Turkey dogs are very helpful in scattering the birds once found. Many times, when a hunter tries to scatter a flock without a dog, all he can accomplish is to scare the turkeys rather than scatter them. In order for the hunter to have a good chance to call the birds back, they must be scattered rather than just scared away.

The well-trained turkey dog that will stay with you while you attempt to call the birds back will be a great asset. If the hunter accidentally wounds a turkey, there is an excellent chance that the dog will be able to chase it down and catch it, saving a lost bird.

The use of a dog to hunt wild turkeys is not a new idea. The turkey dog has been used in some states for at least the past century or more. In Virginia, my home state, hunting turkeys with dogs has a long history. Currently, turkey dogs are legal to use in less than half the states, but their number is increasing as hunting with turkey dogs grows in popularity and acceptance.

This book chronicles my thirty years of fall turkey hunting with dogs and the methods used to train my dogs. While it may seem like there are many stories of birds killed, there were countless other stories where we were unsuccessful.

There are several other specific points that I would like to make very clear. These hunting stories cover my thirty years of hunting with my dogs by myself, with friends, and with family. In all our hunts, everyone who hunts with me always obeys all game laws. We don't hunt out of season or kill more birds than our legal limit. Every bird taken is checked in as required by law. We don't over-harvest an area or a flock of turkeys. My dogs have caught wounded birds that would have been lost otherwise and have never harmed a turkey that wasn't already shot. In my thirty years of fall turkey hunting with dogs, I've seen our turkey populations increase, not decrease. Lastly, all my hunts are made with safety as the top priority.

My hope is that after reading this book, the reader will come away with a better idea of how much the turkey dog can improve his or her fall turkey hunting experience.

THE EARLY DAYS

The first memory I have of seeing wild turkeys was when I was very young. I saw a gang of birds feeding in a clover field behind my house. I was fascinated by the wild turkey and couldn't wait until I was old enough to hunt them. I started turkey hunting with my father in the fall of 1963 when I was eight years old. I hunted several years without any success, but I never lost interest in hunting the wild turkey. I finally killed my first wild turkey during the fall season of 1969. I was hunting with my father when we stumbled into a small gang of turkeys only thirty yards away as they fed along an old dirt road. The birds saw us at about the same time we saw them. They quickly got airborne. I could hear my dad, who was behind me, urging me to shoot. I threw the little .20-gauge to my shoulder and fired. No one was more surprised than I when the turkey fell to the ground in a heap. My first turkey was a nice hen. I was fourteen years old.

It wasn't until the early 1970s that I had my first experience hunting turkeys with dogs. A good friend,

John Stone, and his father, Med Stone, took me hunting with their dogs. Med had two English setters, Queenie and Lady Bird, that he used mainly for grouse hunting. The dogs were trained to point grouse and quail. Med and John quickly found out that Queenie would also trail and flush turkeys. When Queenie flushed turkeys, we would try to get a shot at the birds, if we were lucky enough for them to fly in gun range. Being a good wing shot was a definite advantage in this type of hunting. John, being the better wing shot, had the higher success rate. A large majority of the turkeys we killed in those early years were by this method. If we weren't able to get a good wing shot, we would sit down after the flush and attempt to call the turkeys back into gun range on the ground as they tried to regroup.

There are many good memories I have of fall turkey hunting with John and Queenie. On one occasion, Queenie flushed a gang of turkeys on national forest land high on Sweet Mountain in Alleghany County, Virginia. John was able to kill a bird from that flock as it flew over him. Queenie went to the bird, picked it up, and attempted to retrieve it. This was only natural as Queenie had been trained to retrieve quail and grouse. A wild turkey is a good-sized bird for any dog to try to retrieve, and Queenie was no exception. I'll never forget watching Queenie as she struggled to bring that hefty bird back to John.

There were a number of occasions when Queenie exhibited her skill working turkeys. One such incident took place when John and I had taken Queenie on a hunt on Sweet Mountain. She left us and disappeared down a ridge. We stopped to watch and listen for signs that she had encountered turkeys. A few minutes had passed when we saw a gang of turkeys running back up the ridge in our direction. John and I could see Queenie trotting behind them. She wasn't running hard enough to flush the birds. We couldn't believe what we were seeing. It seemed like she was intentionally herding the turkeys right to us. When the birds got about forty yards away, Queenie picked up the pace and flushed them right toward us. We both fired, and John's shot found the target, killing a nice hen. My shot found only thin air and tree limps. To this day, I still believe that Queenie understood exactly what she was doing by driving those birds to us.

Another memorable hunt with Queenie took place on Mill Ridge, which is also located in Alleghany County. John and I had hunted up the steep side of the ridge to the top where the terrain leveled off. The ridge was covered with a mixture of white and red oak trees that had been dropping acorns for several weeks. We felt that we would find turkeys in this area feeding on these acorns, one of their favorite fall foods. We began seeing large areas where the leaves had been raked away by turkeys scratching for these nuts. The dark soil and damp leaves visible offered proof that we weren't too far from the birds. Queenie's acute nose had picked up their trail as we watched her disappear ahead of us on the horizon. It wasn't long before we heard her barking, and we knew she had found them. Queenie had been a good distance from us when she flushed the birds making it impossible to see which way the birds had flown. In a few minutes, we saw Queenie trotting back to us.

As we approached the area where the turkeys had flushed, John and I heard a young bird calling below us on the north side of the ridge. John said he would take Queenie back down the ridge and hold her as I tried to call the bird in close enough to get a shot. I walked over to a point where the ridge dropped off

Gratten Hepler

sharply and began to call. I made my first call while still standing up, which was a mistake. The bird answered me not fifty yards away and came on a dead run to my call. I saw the bird as it came out from behind a big rock. When I raised my gun to fire, the turkey saw me and turned to run. I took a hurried shot, missing it cleanly. When it started to fly, I shot again, killing the young hen.

This hunt taught me a valuable lesson in my education of turkey hunting. I should have sat down and gotten into shooting position before I made my first call. I had been very fortunate to have a successful end to that hunt.

SALLY

Over the next few years, I was successful hunting in the fall with and without a dog. In the fall of 1975, I decided to get a dog of my own to train. I wanted a breed that was used for bird hunting and was looking for a dog smaller in frame than the English setter. I knew I had several good choices of smaller dogs. I had heard of Springer and Boykin spaniels being used as turkey dogs as well as some breeds of terriers. My dad suggested a Brittany spaniel.

The Brittany spaniel is a smaller-frame dog and is traditionally a close-working dog. In the mountains where I hunt, there are a lot of steep ridges and deep hollows. I felt a close-working dog would be an asset in this type of terrain. The Brittany spaniel is known for being fairly easy to train and willing to please. By nature, the Brittany spaniel is friendly, gentle, and a good family dog in addition to being a good hunting dog. The one drawback was that the Brittany spaniel is a pointing breed. I wanted a dog that would chase and flush turkeys, not point them. The English setter is also a pointing breed and yet Queenie had certainly turned out all right as a turkey chaser. All of these high qualities helped me choose the Brittany spaniel for my choice for a turkey dog. My dad and I started searching for someone with Brittany spaniel puppies for sale. I was lucky to find some in a nearby town. When I went to see the pups, there were three or four left. After looking them over, we picked out a spunky female, and I named her Sally.

Training a turkey dog was something I knew nothing about, and I would need some help getting Sally started in the right direction. John and Med gave me a tremendous amount of assistance on how and when to start training my dog. Sally was only three months old at the time, and they advised not to get into serious training until she was around six months old. At first, I just wanted her to learn and respond to her name. She learned this very quickly. Every day I took her on short walks around the yard. When she would venture a short distance away from me, I would call her back and would drop down on one knee and praise her for coming when called. As time passed, she gained strength and endurance, and our walks increased in length.

To get her used to the sound of a gun, I would carry a BB gun. On our walks, I would stop, make sure she was looking at me, and shoot several times. When Sally was four months old, I started using a .22 rifle to shoot around her. Eventually, I worked up to using a shotgun around her, but I made sure she was at least forty yards away. By gradually building up Sally's tolerance of the noise of a gunshot, I was able to prevent her from becoming gun shy.

When Sally was six months old, I started on other aspects of her training. I had saved both turkey wings from a bird I killed that spring by wrapping them in plastic wrap and freezing them. After letting them thaw out, I tied a string to the wing and pulled it around on the ground. Sally would chase the wing, but I wouldn't let her catch it. I kept these sessions short so I would not tire her out. At six months old, her attention span was still pretty short, and keeping these sessions to a minimum held her attention to the training.

Another method I used was to take Sally inside so that she couldn't see me. I would come back out and drag the turkey wing behind me on the ground, leaving the scent as a trail for her to follow. I would then hide the wing somewhere that wasn't visible. The next step was to let Sally outside and tell her to "hunt a bird." She would follow the trail to where I had hidden the wing. I would also hold the wing over her while she jumped, encouraging her to bark enthusiastically. Praising her at the end of every session helped to increase her confidence and strengthen the bond between us.

The two commands that I felt were most essential were "come" and "stay." To teach her to "come", I started by attaching a check cord to Sally's collar. If she didn't come to me when I called to her, I would gently pull her to me and praise her when she got to me. Knowing that repetition was the best way for her to learn these commands, I tried to work with Sally every day.

Teaching her to stay was next on the agenda. I would put food in her food dish, place her a short distance away from the food, tell her to stay, and then I would walk back to her dish. If she followed me or moved toward the food, I would immediately take her back and tell her to stay again. This was repeated until she knew what the command meant. I didn't allow her to move from the spot I put her in until I told her to come to me.

Over the summer months, I would take Sally to a little-traveled national forest road on Sweet Mountain called the Sweet Road. I would let her out to run in front of the truck. This served two purposes. First, it helped to keep her in good shape. Second, on many of these trips, she would run into turkeys crossing the road. This gave her an opportunity to practice flushing birds just as she would have to do in a hunting situation. After the flush, I would call Sally to me and praise her for her efforts.

These trips over the Sweet Road gave me a chance to try to break some bad habits also. Sally would occasionally run into deer and squirrels that she wanted to chase. When she chased anything other than turkeys, I would scold and spank her. I was careful not to call her back to me and spank her. Instead, I would go to her if she needed to be corrected for something she had done wrong. By going to her, instead of calling her to me to be corrected, I hoped that she would never be afraid to come to me. I knew how important it was to break her of chasing anything other than turkeys. You can't have a good turkey dog that is allowed to run deer or other animals.

When fall finally approached, I was eager to see if the time and effort spent working with Sally, who was now a little more than a year old, would pay off. The first couple of hunting trips were uneventful. Then, one afternoon, John and I were hunting on some private land near Bennett Town Road, which we felt surely held a flock of birds. John and I had hunted up one side of a ridge and down the other side without seeing anything. We had dropped off the ridge into a hollow that bordered on the edge of a field. Sally went out of our sight, and almost immediately, John and I heard turkeys putting loudly (calls given by turkeys when alerted to danger) as they tried to get away from her. We didn't see any of the birds and couldn't tell how many there had been.

Making our way to the edge of the field, John and I crossed a fence at the spot we thought the birds had flushed. We walked along the edge of the field, paused, turned around, and looked back toward the woods. John and I were both startled by the sight of a turkey perched in the top of a cedar tree watching Sally on the ground below. The bird was in gun range, and we both raised our guns and shot almost simultaneously. After the bird crashed to the ground, Sally dived on top of it, pinning it until we got to her. Sally's first turkey was a nice jake.

This had been the perfect situation for a young dog. Getting to grab the turkey while it was still flopping on the ground really served as good training for Sally. John and I praised and petted her for a job well done. I was on cloud nine after this hunt, seeing how well Sally had performed.

November 1977; Sally's first turkey, Gratten, and John

Sally had several more flushes, but no more turkeys would be killed from her that fall. I continued working with Sally through the winter. Her training in the woods took a vacation during the spring. I wouldn't take her in the woods during this time as she might disturb a nesting hen. I didn't want to run the risk of Sally flushing a hen off the nest and having the hen abandon her clutch of eggs. I also was afraid that Sally might get into young poults not yet old enough to fly and possibly wound or kill a poult.

It was during the next season, the fall of 1978, that Sally would show another advantage of hunting turkeys with a dog. One morning in December, several of my friends had joined me on a hunt out on an old logging road that we called the Charlie Wolfe Road. We had gone about a mile when a turkey flushed from a ridge about thirty yards to our right. We were momentarily startled, but two of us got of a shot at

Turkey Dog Tales

the fleeting bird. One of us hit the bird breaking its wing. The turkey went down and hit the ground about seventy-five yards from us and then ran behind a big rock.

Having seen the bird as it went down; Sally was hot on the turkey's trail. As we quickly ran to where the bird had gone down, Sally darted around behind the rock. Almost immediately, we saw the turkey struggling to get to the top of the rock. Sally was right on the bird's tail and jumped up on the rock with it. The wounded bird was attempting to make a hasty escape as it jumped off the rock and started to run. Sally leaped off of the rock right on the turkey's back and grabbed it by the neck. By the time we got to her, Sally had the jake pinned to the ground. We all praised her for catching the wounded bird. If it weren't for Sally staying with the bird and wrestling it down, the jake would have gotten away and died later. A hunter without a good turkey dog would have been helpless in running down and catching the wounded bird as the turkey would have easily outrun the hunter on foot.

It became apparent that all the time I had spent training Sally was beginning to pay off. There was only one problem: every now and then, Sally would take a notion to run deer. She wouldn't bark on the trail but would run the deer as far as she could see it. I tried to break her of this bad habit, but she persisted. I was afraid that this would eventually lead to her either getting shot or lost. Little did I know that my worst fear would soon come to pass.

One morning, I was hunting with my father-in-law, George Filer, behind his house. George and I had been hunting for several hours without finding any birds when Sally suddenly left us. Generally, Sally would leave me for short periods of time while hunting and then check back with me before going out again. After she had been gone for about ten minutes without checking back, I suspected that she had gone after a deer instead of turkeys. Since Sally was unfamiliar with the area we were hunting, I was afraid that she wouldn't be able to find her way back. George and I called for Sally for hours until we could hardly yell anymore. We walked back to George's house, hoping that she had found her way back. I really got worried when she wasn't there. I stayed there until almost dark looking for her.

With my hope of finding Sally fading, I started toward home. My father-in-law lives on Route 18, and I live about ten miles up the same road from him. I was almost home when I came around a turn and saw Sally walking beside the road. She was headed home. I couldn't believe that I had found her. I stopped the truck in the middle of the road and opened the door. As soon as Sally saw me, she ran over and jumped up in the cab. She lay down in my lap and was sound asleep before I could drive the last mile home. I know if I had been a little later she would have beaten me home. After this experience, I renewed my efforts in trying to stop her from running deer. As time would prove, her chasing deer was a habit that I would never be able to completely break her of. The one blessing was that I never lost her again.

Another problem I encountered with Sally, other than running deer, was not being able to keep her with me after the flush. She was much too hyper and rambunctious after the flush to remain still while I attempted to call the birds back. There was no way to hold her still enough that the birds wouldn't see her. I had to take time after a flush to take her back to the truck or back home. This didn't present a problem most of the time. However, sometimes the birds would start calling and trying to reassemble before I could return. If I had another person hunting with me, one of us would hold the dog while the other would try to call a bird in. The drawback to this was that one person was left out of the hunt from this point on. While this worked on several occasions, it was not always the best solution.

Many times, with a long fall turkey season like Virginia has, you will sometimes start the season in late October hunting in a short-sleeved shirt. But in December, you may not be able to put on enough clothes to keep you warm. I remember one such morning when Sally and I were hunting on the Charlie Wolfe Road late in December. It was blowing snow, and temperatures were in the low twenties. I started seeing fresh turkey tracks in the snow. Sally took off, hot on the trail of the birds. I could hear and see the birds as Sally quickly closed the distance. It appeared to be a large flock. I saw several birds that had flown up to the safety of the trees watching Sally as she barked wildly beneath them. As I walked over to get closer to the birds, they saw me and starting flying. I was close enough for a shot and fired three times at the lead bird. I emptied my gun, but never touched a feather.

After all that shooting, I couldn't believe it when I saw one last bird still sitting in a tree watching Sally on the ground below. I dug my last shell out of my pocket and dropped it in the chamber. Just as I raised the gun, the bird flew. I swung ahead of it and fired, dropping the bird. It was a nice-sized hen. I thought to myself that Sally was doing her job, but I wasn't doing so well at mine. I needed to spend some "training time" of my own shooting at clay pigeons. Due to the frigid conditions, I was glad this had been a short hunt that didn't involve sitting down and calling for a long period of time.

Later the same week, after a winter storm had dumped about three more inches of snow on our area, I took Sally to a spot where I thought we might find a gang of birds. It was an area of thick pines surrounded by hardwoods called the Old Home Place. I knew from past experience that the turkeys might head for the pines to feed since the snow wasn't as deep there. Sally and I were walking on an old road that went all the way around the Old Home Place. Sally suddenly went on point and then took off. I was about fifty yards from her when she jumped a small flock of turkeys. They looked like a covey of very large quail as they flushed together. I ran down the road to get a little closer when a bird flew right over my head. It had to be less than twenty yards away. When I tried to stop, I lost my footing on the slick snow. After I regained my balance, I took a shot as one of the birds flew over me. I cleanly missed the bird. The rest of the birds flew in other directions and out of range for me to get another shot. If Sally would have been able to talk, she would have probably given me a hard time about missing that bird. The day didn't end up being a total wash. On the way back to the truck, I killed a turkey that flew out of a tree not far from the site of the original flush. I felt that I had redeemed myself a tiny bit after the earlier fiasco.

In the fall of 1981, I was hunting with a friend, Wayne Lewis, who had never killed a wild turkey. We were hunting on Potts Mountain along an old logging road in an area that was abundant with wild grapes, which turkeys love. We approached an area where the grape vines and mountain laurel were very thick and

Turkey Dog Tales

nearly impossible to see through. Sally disappeared in the tangle with her tail wagging a mile a minute. I knew that she'd picked up some scent, but I thought it may have been a grouse. Suddenly, a turkey flushed out of the brush, flying straight up through the air. As it cleared the trees, it flew directly over our heads. Wayne and I both fired and missed the bird. Wayne fired again, this time killing the nice gobbler. The tom had a nine-inch beard and weighed eighteen pounds. Anyone who says that an old gobbler can't fly with the speed and agility of a grouse hasn't seen one flush with a dog nipping at its tail feathers. One thing for sure, Wayne would never forget his first turkey kill and hunting with Sally.

November 1981; 18-pound gobbler, Wayne's first turkey

Later that same week, John, Wayne, and I were hunting in a different area on Potts Mountain not too far from where Wayne had killed his gobbler earlier.

We had Sally and Queenie along to locate the birds as the two dogs seemed to work well together. We were working our way up the mountain through an oak flat. The flat was bordered by a grown-up clearing that had been cut several years ago. This area also had a stream flowing through it. We knew this was a good location in which to find turkeys. Sally and Queenie were hunting ahead of us when we saw them flush a couple of birds. One big gobbler flew up in a big oak about a hundred yards above us.

The gobbler was watching the dogs bark at him as he sat in the tree. John, Wayne, and I spread out and walked toward the gobbler, knowing that when he saw us coming, he would have to fly out directly over us. This would give one of us a good wing shot at the bird. We started walking toward him while he continued sitting in the tree. We had approached to about fifty yards when he turned on the limb and pitched out of the tree, flying straight up the mountain. He chose the one option that left us without a shot. I've always heard that turkeys will not fly uphill, but this old gobbler proved that theory wrong. All we knew was that he had made his escape to live another day.

On the opening day of the fall season in 1982, Sally and I had been hunting on Sweet Mountain all morning without having any luck. I wanted to make one short hunt before heading in for lunch. As I made my way up toward an old iron-ore mine behind my property, I started to see some fresh scratching that looked like it had been made that morning. Sally started to pick up the fresh scent and took off toward my right in an oak flat. In a few minutes, I could hear Sally barking excitedly. I also heard turkeys clucking and putting. Sally was below me, and I could hear a turkey running in the leaves. I stood still and watched down an old logging road, known as the Ginny Stone Hollow Road, where I figured the bird would cross. It came to the edge of the road and stopped. I fired quickly, thinking it had seen me. At the shot, the turkey dropped, and a small white pine fell over. I hadn't noticed the tree between us, and I was fortunate that enough shot cleared the tree to kill the bird. The turkey was a nice hen, and after closer inspection, I found only a couple of shot in the head and neck. I was very lucky that it ended up being a clean kill.

The very next day, I was on my way to hunt another area on the Sweet Road. I came up over a rise and saw a large gang of turkeys standing in the road. I stopped and backed the truck up so that the turkeys wouldn't see me when I let Sally out. She had already seen the turkeys out of the front window in the truck and took off after them as soon as I let her out of the truck. Sally rushed into the flock, sending them off in all directions. I put Sally back in the truck and went to find a good place to set up to call.

Knowing I needed to get away from the road, I went down the mountain until I was sure that a vehicle traveling on the road wouldn't spook a bird coming to my calling. In about thirty minutes, I heard several young birds starting to call. I knew that if I heard the old hen calling I would have to run her off before the young birds could reassemble with her.

The old hen will usually yelp in long series or cluck excitedly. Young birds, however, will almost always begin their calling with the kee-kee. This is a high-pitched whistle the young birds have used since they were very small. The older they become, the less they use the kee-kee by itself. The hunter then may start to hear the kee-kee run, which is simply several kee-kees combined with one or more yelps.

In this case, the old hen must have been flushed further away because I never heard her call. Several young birds were calling and starting to make their way to me. I tried to imitate the same calls that they were making. I heard a jake giving the typical four-note call of a young gobbler, usually comprised of three kee-kees followed by a raspy yelp or two. He came within twenty yards before I could see him. When his head and neck popped up over a rock, I dropped him. The season was only two days old, and I had used all of my tags.

On several occasions, I had taken my father-in-law, George, turkey hunting. He'd never killed a wild turkey. We managed to get a day when we both could hunt. I told him that I couldn't carry a gun because I didn't have any more fall tags. The shooting would be left up to him. We decided to go to another area on the Sweet Road to hunt. When we started into our chosen spot, we started seeing fresh scratching not far from the road. Sally had already picked up the scent, which she was following into a deep ravine. When she came up the other side, she was running turkeys our way. She had gotten below the turkeys and was running them right to us. When the turkeys saw us standing there, they flushed. One flew over George, and he killed it with one shot from his .20-gauge magnum. The gobbler weighed seventeen pounds and sported a nice eight-inch beard. It had been a quick hunt. I think George thought that fall turkey hunting was easy after this episode. I reminded him that this experience had been the exception and not the rule for most fall hunts.

In the fall of 1983, I took Sally on a hunt behind my house in an area we called Meadow Ridge. This particular morning was very foggy. I worked my way

Turkey Dog Tales

through an old clear-cut and into some big woods where I thought I would find some white oak acorns, which is a favorite food for turkeys. I began to see some fresh scratching made that morning. It wasn't long before Sally picked up the turkey's scent, and I watched as she disappeared into the fog. Suddenly, I heard her barking and could hear excited putting and several wing beats, but I couldn't see which direction the turkeys flew. When Sally returned, it was close to lunchtime so I decided to take her home and come back after a quick lunch.

When I was making my way back after lunch, I could already hear the birds starting to call. The fog hadn't lifted while I was gone. This made it difficult to see past forty yards. I set up with my back to a large oak and began to call. Turkeys would answer me, but they made no attempt to come to my calling. There were several turkeys calling from different locations but all within a hundred yards of each other. They were calling very softly, by using soft yelps and low gobbles. Their gobbles were barely audible unless you knew what to listen for. I had been calling to them for about an hour without making any progress. One gobbler finally worked his way down to my right where I could hear him walking but couldn't see him. He stopped about fifty yards away, just over a little rise. Nothing happened for about fifteen minutes, and I was afraid the turkey had slipped away. The rest of the turkeys had stopped calling. I took the gun off of my knee and just relaxed for a while. I even dozed off for a little nap.

When I woke, it had been about an hour since the birds had stopped calling. I noticed a squirrel was playing in a tree close to where I thought the gobbler had stopped. I watched the squirrel work its way out on a limb. Suddenly, the limb broke, sending the squirrel and the limb crashing to the ground. I then heard something, which I thought was the squirrel, coming toward me in the leaves. Just before it came over the rise into gun range, I realized it wasn't the squirrel but the gobbler running directly toward me. I got my gun up just in time to see the turkey coming. I pulled ahead of the bird and fired. It was a nice gobbler with an eight-inch beard. I couldn't believe that the turkey had stayed in one spot for over an hour without moving. Nor could I believe that the squirrel almost falling on top of the bird would scare the turkey right toward me. There is an old adage that says, "Better to be lucky than good." This hunt certainly fell into that category. I believe that the fog was the main reason the birds were so skittish. Old gobblers are usually in no hurry to regroup, and that was probably another reason that these older birds were taking their good old time.

By now Sally was eight years old, which is middle aged for most dogs, I decided to try to get another Brittany to start training. I also thought that the new pup could gain some valuable experience by hunting with Sally.

MAC

In 1983, I got a male Brittany puppy and named him Mac. I trained him using the same methods I had used to train Sally. Mac showed a much stronger instinct to point than Sally showed during her training. During fall turkey season, I hunted Mac and Sally together, hoping that Mac would learn from Sally. When we did encounter turkeys, Sally usually made the flushes and was a much more aggressive hunter than Mac. I tried hunting Mac by himself, but his results were poor. He hunted at a slow, deliberate pace and always stayed very close to me. Mac finally jumped a gang of turkeys late in the season, and I was able to kill a hen by calling it back. I wanted to hunt him at least one more fall to see if he showed any improvements.

After hunting Mac the next season, he still wasn't aggressive enough to ever be a good turkey dog in my estimation. Since he showed no improvement over the previous year, I decided to try to find him a new home. I thought at the time that Mac would make someone an excellent grouse or quail dog. At this point, I started to look for another dog to train with Sally while I was looking for a good home for Mac.

One of my friends told me he knew an older gentleman who was an avid grouse hunter, and his grouse dog had just passed away. Thinking this might be my golden opportunity to find Mac another home, I called the man. I told him I had a young Brittany spaniel that I had used for turkey hunting but showed a lot of promise as a pointing dog. I told him I would be glad to give Mac to him if would take him. He indicated he would be happy to have him.

The gentleman later told me that he couldn't get Mac to hunt much at first, but after they had time to get used to each other, Mac began hunting a lot better. The man was retired and could hunt Mac almost every day, which eventually paid off as Mac started pointing grouse more frequently. The gentleman told me years later that he had kept Mac until he was fifteen years old, and Mac ended up being one of his better grouse dogs. I was pleased that it had worked out well for both of us and for Mac.

LADY

When I was finally able to locate another litter of Brittany spaniel pups for sale, I selected a female puppy and named her Lady. I used the same basic methods for training Lady as I had for my other dogs. However, I had found out through working with Sally and Mac that these basic methods needed to be modified for each dog's different personality and intelligence level. For example, some dogs must be disciplined less severely than others in order to be broken of the same bad habit. Similarly, other dogs may need extra time and patience devoted to one or more aspects of their training in order to obtain the desired results. As with people, each dog is different.

Early on, I could see Lady was going to be a lot like Sally. She was eager to please and hunted aggressively. Sally was now nine years old, and I could see she was starting to slow down. Even though she was young and inexperienced, Lady didn't mind taking the lead when she got on the trail of turkeys. She showed her energetic nature one summer day when I had taken her for a run on the Sweet Road. I had let her run for several miles before she got tired. I stopped the truck and let her ride in the back. As I rounded a turn, I almost ran over a flock of turkeys in the middle of the road. Lady had seen them through the front window of my shell camper top. I had put the lid down on the camper top when I put her in the back. She ran to the back of the truck bed, hitting the camper top door at full speed and knocking the door open. She proceeded to jump over the tailgate and out of the truck. She hit the ground on a dead run, determined to catch those turkeys. It wasn't long before I heard her barking and the sound of turkeys putting loudly as she charged into the middle of the flock sending them skyward. I knew then that Lady would make a great turkey dog.

On opening day of the fall season in 1985, Lady proved that she was ready and able to take charge. I was hunting with John and another friend, Bert Caul, and we had Sally and Lady with us that morning. We were hunting an area known as Tucker Flats. The forecast had called for heavy rain and a chance of thunderstorms. As we were hunting through an oak flat, we ran into some fresh scratching. Sally and Lady had already picked up the trail as the birds fed up the mountain. Lady raced ahead of Sally as they closed in on the turkeys. I heard both dogs yipping and could see several turkeys flying our way. I could hear the wind whistling through their locked wings as they swiftly glided in our direction. Bert and I swung on one of the birds and fired at about the same time, killing the turkey, a hen. After a few minutes, both dogs came back to us exhausted after their long run up the steep slope. I took the dogs back to the truck and headed

Turkey Dog Tales

back to meet up with Bert and John to see if we could call a turkey back.

It had been drizzling rain all morning. When I got back to Bert and John, it started raining harder and thundering. John told me that he had had enough and was calling it a day. Bert and I decided to stick it out a little longer. We set up and began calling. Little did we know that a bird was closing in on our position as we continued to call. We hadn't been able to hear the bird calling or walking since it was raining and thundering so hard. We finally heard the bird calling below us when it was almost on top of us. Bert waited until the bird, a jake, came to about twenty yards before firing. The young gobbler dropped where he stood. We were both soaking wet and were probably lucky that we hadn't been struck by lightning.

When we got back to the house, my wife, Valerie, was there. She'd come home from work a little before noon. Her business had closed for the day because there was widespread flooding in our county. The roads were flooding and being closed. She told Bert that if he wanted to get back to town and home, he had better leave soon. She took a couple of quick pictures of two soaked hunters with two soaked turkeys and the drenched dogs. Not a pretty picture for sure. Bert and I had good luck, but we were probably two of the few turkey hunters that braved the elements that day.

Later that fall, I was hunting on some land leased by the Bear Wallow Hunt Club known as Moore's Bottom. I had been a member of this hunt club for about thirty years. It wasn't too far from my farm and had some good habitat for turkeys. I took Sally that afternoon after deciding that Lady deserved a rest following an uneventful and long morning hunt. Just after I crossed a branch, Sally picked up the scent of our quarry and took off up a ridge in front of me. She went out of sight, and in a few minutes, I heard her eager barking. Then I saw a couple of big turkeys flying down the ridge. I took her back to the truck and left her while I headed back to the ridge to do some calling. I guessed this had been a small group of gobblers because of the size of the birds I'd seen and the fact that they didn't make any noise when they flushed. Normally, young birds will cutt and putt loudly when they are flushed. Old gobblers, on the other hand, sometimes make very little if any racquet when flushed. I knew I might have a long wait ahead. I positioned myself facing downhill and began my vigil.

It had been about two hours when I heard a gobbler call down the ridge. I called back softly with some gobbler yelps, usually somewhat slower and shorter in number than hen yelping, and he immediately answered. The next time he answered he was definitely closer. After about ten minutes, I could see the gobbler coming up the ridge with his beard swinging. After seeing the bird, I didn't call anymore because I wanted him to have to search for me. I knew that if I called while the gobbler was that close, he would have pinpointed my position immediately. My heart was pounding. The bird came straight to me, and at about twenty yards, I fired, and he dropped at the shot. I jumped up and ran to where he fell. He weighed nineteen and one-half pounds and had a ten-inch beard. He was one of the best fall birds I'd ever killed.

The fall of 1986 started out with great promise. Bert Caul and I were hunting on Snake Run Mountain one afternoon. We had started on top of the mountain and hunted our way over to the south side. Having no luck there, we decided to hunt back on the north

Turkey Dog Tales

side along the top. As we walked along a deer path, Bert and I passed a huge rock that was at least twelve feet high. Lady's pace picked up as if she picked up some scent below the path we were walking on. We stopped and watched as she kept working toward the huge rock. Suddenly, she dashed behind the rock. Jokingly, I said to Bert, "Wouldn't it be funny if Lady jumped a big gobbler from behind that rock?" I had no sooner gotten the words out of my mouth than Bert and I heard a huge commotion coming from that direction. Suddenly, a big gobbler took to the air, trying to escape from the small white and brown predator chasing him. Just as he got to the top of the trees, Bert and I both let drive, and the big bird crashed to the ground. Lady jumped on top of the bird to make sure he wasn't going anywhere. We both looked at each other in disbelief. We'd walked within ten yards of that big rock and the turkey hiding behind it. If it hadn't been for Lady chasing him from his hiding spot, that bird would have sat there and let us walk right on by him.

November 1986; 16-pound gobbler, Bert, and Gratten

Turkey Dog Tales

The very next day, Bert and I decided to go hunting on Potts Mountain. It was raining as we left, but we decided to brave the weather and give it a try anyway. We came to the end of an old road we had been walking on and decided to split up. Bert went up the ridge to my right. Lady and I went up a deep hollow next to the ridge Bert was on. As I worked my way up the rocky hollow, I could see several hundred yards up to my right where Bert had gone. Movement caught my eye, and I could see about six or seven turkeys running up the ridge. They had been able to see me coming in the open timber, and they were intending to make a quick getaway as they worked their way to the top of the ridge.

Lady hadn't seen the turkeys but had picked up their trail and was closing in on them fast. I watched as she disappeared from sight over the top of the ridge. Bert would have the only shot as I was too far down the hollow and out of gun range. I didn't hear Lady bark but soon saw several birds flying down the ridge. I heard Bert shoot but wasn't sure if he had been able to knock one down. I started the long climb up to where he had shot. When I got to the top, stopping to catch my breath, I saw Bert coming with a bird slung over his shoulder. His bird was a nice-sized jake. We decided not to stay and try calling due to the bad weather. We had proven once again that, despite inclement weather conditions, you can still be successful hunting turkeys.

The next day, I was hunting on another piece of land leased by the Bear Wallow Hunt Club. This property was located on the other side of Sweet Mountain in an area known as Castile Run. I had decided to give Lady a well-deserved rest and took Sally on this hunt. I headed out along an old road parallel to the top of the mountain. The road would take me through several deep hollows rich with white oak acorns and grapes. I had seen some old sign but nothing fresh until I got to the last hollow. This hollow was very deep, but the road I was on would allow me to walk quietly right up to the edge where I could see several hundred yards to the bottom of the hollow. As I carefully looked over the edge, I could see a large gang of turkeys scratching in the leaves below me.

The birds had no idea Sally and I were anywhere around as they noisily dug in the dry leaves searching for food. Sally continued running along the road, which wrapped around the hollow in the shape of a horseshoe. She would stop periodically to look into the deep hollow. I knew she could see and hear the birds below her. She finally worked her way to the other side of the birds and then made her move. When the birds saw Sally racing toward them at full speed, they took off running up the ridge right to me. Since Sally had been a good ways from the turkeys when they first saw her coming, they chose to run rather than immediately fly. As they ran by me single file, I picked out a big gobbler, took aim, and fired. He went down and rolled to the bottom of the hollow, ending up in a small creek with Sally on top of him. I had seen John's dog, Queenie, work turkeys like that once, but this was the first time I'd ever seen any of my dogs do this. I could see Sally the whole way, and it sure looked like she had intentionally herded those birds to me just as Queenie had done on a hunt several years ago.

This would be one of Sally's last hunts. Sally was twelve years old, and she unfortunately developed hip problems. She had been a loving companion and faithful hunting dog. Sadly, I had to have her put down. She'd been in a lot of pain, and I knew it was the right thing to do, but that didn't make it any easier. When thinking of Sally, I always think of this unforgettable hunt.

During this time, I was glad to have Lady. She helped to take my mind off of losing Sally. Lady was now three years old and had proven she was a fine turkey dog. But Lady had the same flaw that had plagued Sally throughout her life. Every now and then, she would run deer. I had tried scolding and whipping her, but she still wasn't completely broken of this bad habit. I would just have to continue working with her even though I knew it would be hard to break her at her age.

In the fall of 1987, I was hunting with my cousin from northern Virginia. He'd never killed a turkey and was eager to give fall hunting a try. I explained how we would attempt to use Lady to locate a flock of turkeys and what we would do after the gang had been split up. We were hunting behind my house on a combination of private and national forest land on Sweet Mountain. Lady had jumped turkeys in this area earlier in the year, but we hadn't killed any birds from that flock. There were plenty of acorns in that area, and I felt that we might find those birds again. When we got to the area, Lady left us and disappeared around the side of a ridge. We weren't in a good spot by being down in a low area between two ridges. If Lady flushed turkeys, there would be a good chance we wouldn't hear her or see the birds when they flew. As we waited, I finally saw a turkey flying around the ridge where Lady had gone.

The bird flew too high for a shot. It lit in a large white pine about a hundred yards above us. I told my cousin to keep his eye on the bird and walk straight toward it. I told him that more than likely the bird would see him coming and fly out, heading downhill right over him. This should give him a good shot. Sure enough, the bird bailed out and flew over my cousin. He fired, hitting the bird but not killing it. As it lost altitude, it flew directly over me. I was able to get off a shot and brought him down. The jake hit the ground just as Lady came back to us. My cousin was tickled to even see a bird much less kill one.

The 1988 hunting season began when, a good friend of mine, Tad Robertson, and I decided to go out on Sunday afternoon, opening day eve, with Lady and try to split up a gang before dark. Of course, we didn't take a gun. If we were successful, we would go back early on opening day with a better chance of calling a bird in. Tad and I took at least one week of vacation time from work to turkey hunt together during the fall season. This was the start of what would become a tradition for Tad and me.

It was late in the afternoon when Lady started "making game." The phrase "making game" refers to the dog picking up some scent and becoming noticeably excited by wagging its tail excitedly. It wasn't long before Lady trailed the turkeys to a steep ridge near the Sweet Road. Lady charged into the gang, scattering them in all directions. My hopes soared as I felt we should at least hear some birds calling the next morning.

Before daylight on opening day, Tad and I were back where we had jumped the birds the day before. The only problem we had was that during the night, the wind had picked up and now was gusting. This made it extremely difficult to hear. We knew that turkeys sometimes don't respond well on windy days. As the woods began to lighten, I thought I heard a kee-kee from a young bird between the gusts of wind.

Turkey Dog Tales

I called back louder than I normally would to make sure the bird heard me over the wind. The young hen answered my call aggressively. I shifted my position slightly to have a better shot if the bird came as I thought it would. The bird came quickly, anxious to join up with one of her siblings. I caught a glimpse of the bird as it came toward my position. Suddenly, she turned and was going to come further to my right. I shifted, quickly getting ready. I could now hear the bird walking, but the wind made it hard to tell exactly where she would pop out of the brush. The hen showed up at ten yards. I knew I would only have a split second to make my move. I swung my gun around, aimed, and shot in one quick motion, killing the turkey. I was very lucky the young hen didn't see me and flush. We weren't able to call any more birds as the wind continued to get stronger as the day went on. This hunt had been an exciting start to the season that was now all of an hour old.

Things don't always go as planned in turkey hunting. For every successful hunt, there must be at least a dozen where something goes wrong or where you simply don't encounter any birds. A good example would be a hunt Lady and I went on late in the fall of 1988 on the Charlie Wolfe Road. Lady had flushed a small gang of gobblers about mid-morning. When Lady jumped the birds, I could see beards on several of the birds as they flew. I'd already killed a bird that fall, so I took Lady back to the house and got my dad to go back with me. I was hoping he might get a chance at getting a bird. When we arrived at the flush site, I put my dad about fifty yards below the road, and I got in position twenty yards behind him. It had been about an hour since the birds had been split, and we hadn't heard any calling. I decided to do some gobbler yelping with my mouth call, hoping to get a response. I called about every ten minutes or so for about an hour. We didn't hear a peep. This hadn't come as too much of a surprise. Sometimes old gobblers may attempt to get back together quickly, but more often, they can take as long as several days to reassemble.

Without hearing any birds, I figured my dad's patience was wearing thin. I knew mine was. I got up and walked down to my dad to see if he was getting tired. He said he was ready to start back to the truck. The road we had come in on was very muddy. After walking about ten yards, I noticed turkey tracks that hadn't been there when we had come in. I followed the tracks about fifty yards to where a ridge came up and met the road. The tracks first appeared at that ridge, went out to right above where we had been sitting, and then went back the other way. I told my dad that I believed the old bird heard me calling, came silently up the ridge next to us, walked out on the road, saw me, turned around, and left without making a sound. It makes you wonder how many times this happens and there are no telltale tracks left behind. That crafty gobbler had outsmarted me on that hunt. He'd won that particular battle, but my dad reminded me, "That's what makes turkey hunting so much fun."

Another good example of a hunt that certainly didn't go as planned was one I took that same fall with a good friend, Dwain Tyree. Dwain and I had done a lot of spring hunting together, but we hadn't done that much fall turkey hunting. We were hunting on the Bear Wallow Hunt Club land on Castile Run. As soon as we got out of the truck that morning, we heard birds calling on the ridge above our position. I told Dwain I would let Lady out to go after the birds and flush them. She immediately heard them calling and hadn't gone a hundred yards before birds were going everywhere. Dwain and I quickly got to the flush site. Turkeys were sitting in the trees with Lady barking at them. They were so busy watching her that they hadn't seen us coming. Dwain shot at one bird sitting in a tree, missing the bird cleanly. With his shot, the other birds spooked, and they quickly departed. I told Dwain that we shouldn't have any trouble calling a young bird in from this large gang.

After an hour had passed without hearing anything, I started calling. I kept thinking it was only a matter of time until we'd be able to call in a bird. By late afternoon, I wasn't thinking that anymore. We had sat there all day and never heard a bird call. I still haven't figured out what happened to those birds, but they had managed to elude us that day.

Gratten Hepler

BABE

Since Lady was now five years old, I felt that it was time to get another dog and start training it to be ready to take over as Lady got older. I started watching the paper in hope of finding another pup. I saw an ad for German shorthair pups. I wasn't really interested in getting a dog that size, but I decided to at least go look at the puppies. The man selling them looked at me like I was crazy when I told him I intended to train this pup to hunt turkeys. I finally decided, despite my reservations, to get one of the puppies. After looking them over, I chose a female and named her Babe. I started her training just as I had with my other dogs. After six months of working with her, I hoped that Babe would be far enough along in her training to be able to hunt with Lady during the upcoming fall season.

The summer months were spent running Babe with Lady, chasing turkeys on the Sweet Road. Babe learned quickly and was ready for her rookie season. I had tried to train Babe to stay with me in a blind after the flush. Unfortunately, she was even more hyper

Turkey Dog Tales

than Lady or Sally had ever been. Babe couldn't be still long enough to sit down, much less lie down and be still in a blind. I knew I would have to treat her just like Lady and Sally by taking her back to the truck or back home after a flush.

The first couple of days of the next fall season were uneventful. We did a lot of walking with no luck until Thursday afternoon of the first week. That morning started out wet with heavy rain. After lunch, the rain quit, but it was very foggy. I made up my mind to take the dogs and see what we could find. With the ground being damp from the rain and no wind, conditions would be good for the dogs to pick up scent and locate a flock of turkeys.

I decided to hunt on land behind my house on Sweet Mountain. Not long into the hunt, I watched as Babe and Lady's tails started going like crazy, indicating they were picking up scent. I stopped and watched them disappear into the fog. It wasn't long before I heard the birds putting. The fog kept me from seeing any of the birds, but it sounded like a big gang by all the commotion. Within a few minutes, Babe and Lady came back, and I gave both some well-deserved praise. After taking the dogs back home, I returned to the flush site. I would wait there until dark and try to prevent the birds from getting back together. I waited until dark without hearing any calling. I believe that if it hadn't been for the fog, the birds would have tried to reassemble before dark.

That night, I called Bert and Tad to set up a morning hunt. Tad said Dwain wanted to go too. I knew that we would have to split up with four hunters in the woods. The next morning, each of us took a different spot close to where the turkeys had flushed the day before and set up, waiting for daybreak. It hadn't gotten light enough to see well when I heard birds calling from their roost trees below me. The fog wasn't as bad as it had been the day before. I hoped the birds would be eager to get back together after having spent the night alone. I tree-called, which is soft yelping made by turkeys still on the roost, to the birds. The birds and I carried on a conversation for a few minutes. I got a rude awakening when I saw one of the birds pitch out of the tree and head straight for me on the wing. It appeared that it was going to land right on top of me. I brought the gun to my shoulder and fired just before it landed, killing the jake. As things calmed down, I heard other birds calling, and I knew chances were good that someone else would get a shot. Before the morning was over, both Tad and Dwain called in and killed jakes. We gave Bert a pretty hard time since he was the only one that didn't put a tag on a bird that morning.

November 1989; three jakes killed from a Lady-and-Babe flush, Gratten, Tad, and Dwain

Turkey Dog Tales

Later that fall, I made several more hunts with Babe only. She hunted well, but at times, she would hunt too far away from me. She would take off and go as much as a half a mile away. Babe might have jumped birds while she was gone, but I wouldn't know it with her hunting that far away. She might have been two or three ridges away or maybe in the bottom of a hollow where I couldn't hear her bark or hear birds putting as they flushed. Much of the terrain I hunt is steep and mountainous. A close-working dog, as I had found out the hard way, was a better choice than one that hunted as far away as Babe did. By hunting Babe with Lady, I could somewhat control Babe's range because Lady worked close to me, and Babe never ventured far from Lady.

A good example of this took place in December 1990. I was hunting near the top of Sweet Mountain. After hunting through an oak flat with no success, I headed for the top of the mountain. I started back on the south side of the mountain where I had seen more sign. Babe stayed with Lady, which I was happy to see. I didn't want Babe hunting down the other side of the mountain because I wouldn't have known if she got into turkeys. About mid-morning, I noticed Babe and Lady making game. Abruptly, both dogs started heading straight away from me at a high rate of speed. Soon, I heard their barking and saw six or eight big turkeys flying in all directions off the mountain. Being close to the top of the mountain when they were flushed, the birds were able to set their wings and glide a long way to the valley below. I had a long way back to the truck, and by the time I got home, it was time for lunch. If I was right, it would probably be a while before these gobblers tried to regroup as they had a long walk back up the mountain. I got back to the flush site by early afternoon. I got settled in for what I thought might be a long afternoon.

Roughly every fifteen minutes, I called using raspy gobbler yelps and clucks. I had been there about an hour when I heard something making a strange noise coming from the other side of the mountain. I wasn't sure what I was hearing. I heard it again, closer this time, and it sounded like a raven calling. Finally, I realized that what I was hearing was an old gobbler trying to get a response from one of his buddies. His yelping had been so raspy and deliberate that I almost hadn't recognized the call as being made by a turkey. I began calling back, trying to imitate his raspy calls as closely as I could. He called again and was closer. I finally saw him coming when he was about fifty yards from me searching for his lost buddy. If he came another twenty yards, he would be in good range of my .12-gauge. He closed the distance quickly, and when he gave me an open shot, I fired. He dropped in his tracks. It was late afternoon by then. It had been about six hours since the flush. The bird weighed sixteen and one-half pounds and had a nine-inch beard.

Hunting with Babe alone was frustrating at times. I was still having the same problem with her hunting too far away from me. Lady was now seven years old, and I knew that she wouldn't be able to keep up with Babe many more seasons. I continued hunting Babe through the fall of 1991. Later that same year, I met a gentleman at the state meeting of the National Wild Turkey Federation in Charlottesville, Virginia, who was looking for a turkey dog. I told him about Babe and explained that the only problem I had with her was that she would hunt too far from me. He said that he hunted in eastern Virginia, and the territory he hunted was relatively flat. He felt like her style of hunting wouldn't be as much of a problem for him as it had been for me. He went on to say that if I was willing to sell her, he would like to have her and continue working her on turkeys. About six months after I had sold her, I saw the gentleman again at another NWTF meeting, and he said that he had been very happy with her. I was glad that Babe had found a good home and was still able to hunt turkeys.

Gratten Hepler

LADY (Part 2)

Now I was back to hunting with one dog. I missed Babe as a hunting companion but knew she was in a better situation. In the fall of 1993, Tad and I went out again on opening day eve to scout for turkeys. Right before dark, Lady flushed a gang in almost the same spot she had found turkeys on several previous hunts in different years. This had been a lucky spot for us and was less than two hundred yards from the Sweet Road. Once again with Lady's help, we had our opening morning set. Tad and I both had a feeling of *déjà vu* when we arrived back the next morning. This was at least the third time we'd been at that exact same spot on opening morning with a gang split up from the night before. As it began to get light, we could hear several birds calling in the distance. Tad and I both started calling. A bird on Tad's side of the ridge came running to his calling, and he killed the hen cleanly. We stayed in hope of getting another bird fired up, but Tad's bird turned out to be the only one for that day.

Turkey Dog Tales

Tuesday proved to be uneventful. On Wednesday, we decided to try the same spot where Tad had killed his bird the first day. We wanted to see if there might be a bird still split off from the gang that Lady had jumped on Sunday. It was a long shot, but it was worth a try. Tad and I split up on either side of the ridge and started to call. We hadn't been there long before I got an answer from a ridge to my left. The bird was on its way in short order and answered me every time I called. It sounded like an adult hen yelping as she continued to rapidly close the distance. I knew when it got there it was going to pop up right in front of me. I'd purposely set up using the terrain to my advantage so that when I could see the bird, and it could see me, it would be in gun range.

Many times, a turkey will be reluctant to come in if it can see your calling position from a distance but can't see another turkey. The bird might then "hang up," or stop out of gun range. There is a downside of setting up so that the turkey will be in gun range when you see it. You have to be able to accurately judge where the turkey will show up so that you have your gun ready and pointing in the right direction. If, for instance, the leaves are wet, making it hard to hear the bird walking, it becomes difficult to be prepared when it shows up unexpectedly. At close range, a turkey will instantly see you move your gun and run or fly, offering only a poor shot or no shot at all.

When I finally saw her, she was only seven steps away. I didn't have a completely clear shot as there were some small branches and leaves in my line of fire. At seven yards, I was pretty sure it wouldn't be a problem. I also knew that I had better be dead on target because my pattern from my full choke .12-gauge would be about the size of a tennis ball at that close range. My shot was true. The bird was a nice adult hen. Even though it had been a couple of days since this bird had been flushed, she was anxious to get back with her group. Many times, even young turkeys may take longer to regroup if they were shot at several times or perhaps hunting pressure from other hunters kept them from getting back together sooner.

Sometimes in fall hunting, if you are successful in splitting up a group of young birds, the old hen will be able to call all or most of her young back together quickly despite your best efforts to keep her from doing so. If you hear her calling, you have two options. One is to go to her and run her off as quickly as you can. The other is to mark the spot where they got back together and take the dog to that spot with the hope of splitting them up again. You have virtually no chance at calling the birds in once the old hen has started calling. Those young birds know her voice over all others and will go quickly and instinctively to her. Once they are back together, they normally stop calling and leave the area quickly.

In the fall of 1993, I had a situation like this. I was hunting with a friend of mine, Jimmy Sprouse. We were hunting in Moore's Bottom one morning when Lady flushed a gang of young birds. We set up on a small finger ridge where the turkeys had flushed. I set up behind Jimmy and held Lady. After about an hour, having heard no calling, I began to kee-kee in an effort to get a response. The old hen started yelping loudly about two hundred yards away on another finger ridge. I made the mistake of trying to call like her. Several young birds were kee-keeing back, but they weren't headed our way. Within ten minutes, they went right to the old hen. They stopped calling, and I knew they had regrouped.

Turkey Dog Tales

When Lady heard the birds calling, she was anxious to go after them. I turned her loose with the hope of splitting them up again. Lady made a beeline for the ridge where the turkeys had regrouped, and it wasn't long before she had them split up once again. We set up one more time. Once again, I put Jimmy ahead of me facing down the ridge. We hadn't been there long before I heard a turkey kee-keeing on the other side of a little branch. This time, the old hen was silent. I kept up the turkey talk with the young bird, and it headed steadily our way. I knew that by the time the bird got to where I was, it would have to walk right past Jimmy, offering him a good shot. At the sound of the gun going off, Lady went to the downed bird, but she didn't have to chase this bird. We knew that we would have never been able to catch up to and re-flush those birds had we not had a good turkey dog. Jimmy had a fine young hen to fix for Thanksgiving dinner in a couple of weeks.

In all successful turkey hunts, whether in the spring or fall, some luck is involved. We had a hunt in 1995 that showed that a little luck can go a long way. I was hunting with my father-in-law, George, and Lady on Potts Mountain. George and I had hunted up a rocky hollow with Lady ahead of us. We were going to cross over a ridge to hunt down another hollow on our way back to the truck. When we reached the top of the ridge, I could see turkeys busily scratching below us. Lady hadn't seen or winded them yet, but she was hunting her way toward them. She finally winded them from above and ran down the hollow. They heard her coming in the leaves and started running up another ridge through some thick laurel. Lady finally caught up to them, sending them flying down the mountain. I told

George that I would take Lady back to the truck and meet him back there in about thirty minutes.

When I returned, George and I decided to work our way to the top of the ridge where the birds had flushed. Neither one of us had been to the top of this ridge before. We started up the steep brushy ridge toward our destination. We had gone about halfway when we stopped to catch our breath. I heard something in the leaves walking toward us. We both dropped to our knees, having nowhere to hide. I saw two gobblers coming about thirty yards from us. George must have seen them too as he shouldered his gun, picked out a clear spot to shoot through, and fired, killing the bird instantly. Why those birds didn't see us I will never know. I never made the first call but, instead, believe the gobblers had heard us walking in the leaves and thought we were a couple of their lost buddies. I have heard people say that turkeys won't go into thick brush. These two birds certainly proved that statement to be wrong. Stopping when we had and having the birds walk right in on top of us without them seeing us was pure luck. George killing an old gobbler on the last day of the season fit into that same category. The gobbler weighed eighteen pounds and sported a nine-inch beard.

Sadly, Lady would develop the same hip problems that had plagued Sally. Lady got worse over the spring and summer. Seeing her suffer in warm weather, I knew she would be in tremendous pain when cold weather set in. She was twelve that summer when I had her put down.

The fall of 1995 and 1996 I hunted without a dog. Even though I was able to kill a bird both years, it just wasn't the same without a dog. I missed watching the dog hunt, and I missed working with them during the off season. Most of all, I missed their companionship. I knew then that I didn't want to hunt another fall turkey season without a turkey dog.

JENNY

The search for another dog began in early 1996, but it would be late that same year before I was able to locate a litter of Brittany spaniel puppies. The gentleman that had the pups told Valerie and me that his male dog that was registered with the AKC and one of his females that was registered with the AFD had accidentally been bred. Since the two organizations don't recognize each other's puppies as purebred, the pups of this litter couldn't be registered. All four of my previous dogs were purebred AKC-registered dogs. While I had some reservations, Valerie did not. The man selling the pups and only had two left and told us we could have both of them for the price of one. Valerie was so taken with the pups that she thought it was a good idea to get both of them.

It was late November and very cold. I had always kept my hunting dogs outside in a pen. They weren't allowed in the house for any reason. I had always been told that you can't make a hunting dog a pet. Making a hunting dog a pet would ruin the dog for

Turkey Dog Tales

hunting. Valerie argued that if we got both, they would keep each other warm outside in the pen. I decided on just one of the females because I didn't think I could handle training both dogs at the same time. The one that Valerie and I picked out was a very energetic and bright-eyed little female. We named her Jenny.

When we got Jenny home, it was bitter cold and windy. Valerie refused to leave her out in the pen. I didn't think much of this and was afraid that Valerie would ruin Jenny by trying to keep her inside. Valerie became so attached to Jenny that she slept with her in the den. Jenny would crawl up on Valerie and lie down around her neck, and they would sleep like that. I don't think Jenny ever spent a night outside after that. She was a pet and a turkey dog from the moment we got her home. Little did I know, Jenny, the "pet," would become the best turkey dog I ever owned. Most bird hunters know that if you get one good bird dog in your life you are very lucky. With Jenny, I was more than lucky. She ended up becoming my best turkey dog and a true family member.

It was the spring of 1997, and Jenny was now about six months old. She was very intelligent and her training was going very well. I had gone through her obedience training as well as worked her with a turkey wing from a gobbler I killed in the spring. One morning, I had taken her for a walk behind my house. She suddenly took off after something and starting barking. I soon realized that she had jumped a deer and was in hot pursuit.

Luckily, the deer turned and started running back toward me where I could hopefully intercept Jenny as she ran by. Since I had trouble with both Sally and Lady in this regard, I was determined to stop this bad habit right then. When the deer ran past me, I stepped into the path and waited for Jenny to come by. After catching her, I scolded and whipped her. Needless to say, she stayed behind me with her tail tucked between her legs all the way home. I hoped that by catching her in the act at this young age, this experience would help to break her of running any more deer. Only time would tell for sure.

In July, I felt like most of the young turkeys could fly by then, so I decided to take Jenny around the edges of fields where we might find some birds feeding on insects. One day, as I had Jenny out walking through a field, I noticed her tail started going back and forth like crazy. With her nose to the ground, she followed the trail out of my sight. I hoped that it was turkeys. In a few minutes, I knew that it was. I could hear them flying and calling excitedly. This was her first experience with turkeys, and when she came back to me, I noticed she was carrying something in her mouth. I knelt down when she came over to me, and Jenny proudly spit a turkey poult out on the ground. As soon as she did, the frightened little bird took off back down the hill as fast as its little legs would carry it. I grabbed Jenny to make sure she didn't take off after the little bird again. I praised and petted her for finding the birds. The bird must have been part of a late hatch and less than two weeks old as most poults can fly after that age.

During the summer months, Jenny was able to find and flush several more flocks, but each time I noticed that she never barked as she flushed the birds. After thinking about it for a while, I remembered the scolding and spanking she got when I caught her running and barking after that deer. I think she remembered it also because she hadn't run a deer since then, but she hadn't barked either. I would have to learn to live with this tradeoff. I was hopeful that Jenny's not barking wouldn't be a big deal. She generally hunted close enough to me that I could tell when she was on turkeys. When she had flushed gangs over the summer, I had been able to see the birds as they flushed or at least hear them putting excitedly. More important, I was glad that she wasn't chasing deer.

After a flush, I had always wanted to keep my dog with me in a blind. I had tried to train my other dogs to stay with me but had been unsuccessful so far. The training method I most often employed would be to take the dog for a run on the Sweet Road during the summer and early fall. If a gang was scattered by the dog, I would take it to the spot where the turkeys had been flushed and sit down. I would leash the dog, telling it to stay in an effort to keep it with me while it calmed down. None of my previous dogs were calm enough to stay with me without spooking the turkeys that might come back to my calling. I had found out after working with my other turkey dogs how hard it was to train a dog to stay with you and remain still and quiet after the flush. Training and encouraging your turkey dog to hunt aggressively is hard enough. Try to imagine the difficulty in telling the dog immediately after the flush it must now lie down and remain motionless. The dog might have to endure a long wait while staying quiet and stationary while having to listen to turkeys calling and walking around in the leaves.

Being able to keep the dog with me would have meant a lot less time spent walking back and forth to the truck or back home. It would also mean that if a bird was wounded by the hunter, there would be a good chance the dog would catch the bird before it could escape. I had witnessed birds that were wounded and escaped. This was due in part because I had to take the time to go back and get the dog and bring her back to where the bird had been wounded. This meant that the scent, in all probability, would be gone. I'd never been successful in finding a wounded bird under these circumstances. In working with Jenny, she had showed promise that she might be the dog that I had been searching for and would stay with me while I called the birds back. Little did I know then that my very first hunt with Jenny would validate my hopes of having a faithful companion while calling turkeys.

In the fall of 1997, Tad, Rob Tyree, and I were hunting behind my house. We had hunted all morning without having any luck. By chance, we became separated, and Jenny and I started hunting our way back to the truck on the edge of an old field. I was walking back when I thought I heard a turkey call. I stopped to listen to see if the turkey would call again. Seconds later, I heard the turkey repeat its call. Jenny hadn't flushed any birds, so I wasn't sure if the turkey that was calling was alone or part of a gang. I quickly sat down and got into shooting position and noticed that while I was settling down, Jenny had stopped hunting and had lain down beside me. I began answering the turkey's calls, and it wasn't long before I could see the bird working its way through the field. I didn't think Jenny was aware that the tom was coming because she couldn't see it from were she lay and was unable to hear it because it was walking in the tall grass. I hoped she wouldn't hear the gobbler calling as it came in because I was afraid she would jump up at the last minute and spook the bird. When it was in gun range, I quickly aimed and fired. Jenny jumped up and ran eagerly toward the turkey, reaching the bird while it still flopped on the ground. The gobbler had an eight-and-a-half-inch beard and weighed fifteen pounds. The bird certainly acted as though he had been split from a gang. I will never know for sure. After this episode, my hope soared of finally having a dog that would stay with me during the calling process.

A week later, I was hunting with Jenny on a cool and clear afternoon on the Bear Wallow Hunt Club land on Castile Run. I had crossed an old power line and headed up a logging road, which would take me through several hollows and small finger ridges. I'd seen scratching in the road before the season came in. I started seeing some fresh sign near the last hollow on the hunt-club property. Jenny's excitement level picked up as she vanished, sprinting up the ridge in hot pursuit. After a couple of minutes, I saw several turkeys fly near the top of the mountain about a quarter-mile away. The last bird I saw fly started straight off the mountain and then in mid-flight turned and started coming back directly toward me. I stood still and watched as the bird gracefully glided, dropping altitude as it came. I couldn't believe it as it came to rest in the top of a big red oak right beside me. I could see a nice beard swinging from the bird's chest. I could hear Jenny coming back, and I saw the gobbler in the tree looking her way watching her. I took the opportunity while the bird was distracted to raise my gun and fire. It hit the ground and rolled down a steep embankment to the bottom of the hollow. Jenny, hearing all the commotion, ran up and saw the bird flopping in the leaves and grabbed the turkey.

Gratten Hepler

November 1992; Jenny's first turkey, a nice 17-pound gobbler

These turkeys had been above me several hundred yards away, and had it not been for Jenny, I would never have been able to catch up to them and make a flush. It would have been almost impossible for anyone to run and catch these birds as they ran uphill, much less scatter the birds effectively. But the turkeys couldn't outrun Jenny. This was an excellent example of why a dog is so valuable in flushing turkeys.

Several times during the two years that I was hunting without the benefit of a dog, I had seen turkeys at a hundred yards or less. I tried to run after them to flush them, but in every case, they ran from me and escaped without my being able to scatter them. This was the first flush and kill that Jenny would get credit for. The combination of Jenny getting to see the bird fall from the tree and getting to jump in on top of it was great for her training. My praising her would help to confirm that everything she had done was right. The

Turkey Dog Tales

gobbler weighed seventeen pounds and had a seven-inch beard. Not bad for Jenny's first bird.

Turkeys sometimes act entirely differently than the way you think they are supposed to. While turkeys have certain tendencies that they follow, they will still pull out a new trick from time to time. You can hunt turkeys all of your life and still learn something new. In most cases, turkeys that are flushed and scattered in the fall will return to the spot where they were flushed. While this is true most of the time, there are exceptions to this rule.

In the fall of 1998, Jenny had flushed a gang of turkeys late one afternoon close to the Sweet Road. Jenny and I were back the next morning and set up right at the flush site. Right after daybreak, I heard an old hen calling on the next ridge about a quarter-mile away. She had decided on a different spot to get her flock back together than where they had been flushed. Knowing I didn't have long to make a move, Jenny and I took off toward her in an effort to scare her off. She heard us coming and quit calling. Jenny continued the pursuit until she flushed the hen off the ridge top. I slipped in close to where the old hen had been and began calling. In less than five minutes, I called in and killed a young hen. Why the old hen chose a different spot to reassemble her flock will always remain a mystery to me. I have encountered this behavior a lot more in recent years.

A few days later, Tad, Rob, and I were looking to get Rob his first turkey. We were hunting in Moore's Bottom where I had seen turkey signs earlier. We were hoping to catch the birds in a long hollow with a stream flowing down the length of the hollow. This hollow was full of white oak acorns, giving the turkeys ready access to one of their favored foods. We started to see some fresh scratching as the turkeys had fed up a ridge to our left. Jenny followed the fresh sign up the ridge, flushing the birds as she neared the top. The ones we could see flew down the top of the ridge. We climbed to the top and found a good setup. I put Rob facing down the ridge about forty yards ahead of Jenny and me. Soon, we heard a bird calling, and I answered back.

Every time the bird called, I could feel Jenny shaking underneath the camo cloth draped over her. I had a tight hold on her in order to keep her from jumping up and spooking the bird. The bird finally showed up but came in to our right. Rob had to swing and shoot quickly. When Rob shot, the bird took off running, dragging a wing, indicating the wing had been broken. Jumping up immediately, Jenny saw the bird running and took off after it. The bird crossed a hollow and ran up the other side of a ridge. Jenny caught up to it about halfway up the ridge, grabbing the bird. Rob and I could see both Jenny and the bird rolling down the hill in a blur of black and white, fur and feathers. We caught up to them at the bottom of the hollow where they had stopped. The bird's broken wing hadn't stopped it from running a quarter-mile before Jenny caught it. Rob and I both knew that if it weren't for Jenny, that bird would have been long gone.

Turkey Dog Tales

October 1998; Rob's first turkey, Gratten, Rob, and Tad

New Year's Day 1999 arrived with three inches of snow on the ground. My son, Ben; my neighbor and friend, Todd Fix; and I decided to take Jenny out and see what we could find. Ben had killed a nice spring gobbler several years ago on Todd's hunt club land, and we wanted to return the favor. We started seeing tracks in the snow and bare leaves turned up by the turkeys' scratching. Jenny had picked up their scent and quickly tracked the birds down, scattering them in several directions. We set up after the flush and began calling. We heard several birds calling, but one was especially eager and was headed our way. The bird came straight to Todd like he was on a string. Todd was carrying a scoped .22 magnum. At his shot, the bird went down but was quickly up and running back down the ridge. Jenny sprang from underneath her camouflage cloth and sprinted after the bird. She disappeared over a rise and down a narrow hollow filled with pine trees that had been blown down during a recent storm. By the time we caught up with Jenny, she had the turkey down. It looked like it had tried to crawl underneath a brush pile in an effort to hide. We knew that without Jenny, our chances of finding that wounded hen would have been slim.

January 1999; another wounded turkey caught by Jenny on a cold winter day, Todd, Gratten, and Ben

Turkey Dog Tales

The first fall season for Jenny had proved to be very rewarding with fourteen flushes and four kills to her credit. She had caught two of the four birds killed that fall. Both turkeys, having been wounded, would have escaped had it not been for Jenny.

A large majority of the time in the fall, you will be hunting young birds of the year. But occasionally, you get lucky and get a flush of old gobblers. If you are really lucky, you may get them scattered in different directions and have an opportunity to call one back. In 1999, Jenny flushed a gang of old gobblers first thing on opening morning. The birds, when flushed, had been feeding near a small creek located in Moore's Bottom. I didn't want to set up in the bottom, thinking the birds would try to regroup on the adjacent ridge, known as Hickory Hill. Tad, Rob, and I headed off in that direction along with Jenny. When we made it to the top of the ridge, we set up quickly and began to call.

Roughly an hour later, around mid-morning, we finally heard one of the gobblers answer our call from the next ridge over, known as Leading Ridge. Another bird started calling and gobbling further up the ridge. He wasn't gobbling to call in a hen as in the spring but rather to get back with his bachelor buddies. They didn't want to budge from their spot on the ridge. Tad, Rob, and I finally heard another bird calling behind us. After I made another call, we heard him answer again, but this time he was closer. The birds on Leading Ridge continued to call as well. When the bird behind us showed up, Tad was ready for him and dropped him with one well-placed shot. After several minutes of congratulations and admiring the bird, the turkeys on Leading Ridge continued yelping and gobbling.

Tad's shot hadn't spooked the birds since they were a quarter-mile away.

While I attempted to circle around the birds on Leading Ridge, Rob and Tad had said they would stay there in an effort to call in another bird for Rob. By the time I got over to the ridge where they had been calling, the birds had gone silent. I decided to call to see if I could get them fired up again. I got an immediate answer from above me. One bird yelped while the other bird gobbled. I picked up the pace of my calling with loud gobbler yelps and clucks. They really got excited when they heard my calls but still wouldn't head my way. The gobblers had another destination in mind as they were going away from me up the mountain.

Time to move again, I thought. I circled around the birds, calling each time I stopped. They would answer me every time I called. I could keep track of their position by using this tactic. I finally got in front of them and picked out a spot to call from. I started calling one more time with my mouth calls as well as my slate call, trying to sound like several birds. The birds were going crazy with their yelping, cutting, and gobbling. It sounded like a spring hunt with all the excited calling. Using my mouth call, I started cutting, issuing a challenge to the boss gobbler. That did the trick as he cut back to me loudly, this time getting closer. My gun was up and ready when he appeared about thirty yards away. I let drive with a load of #5 shot, and the gobbler hit the ground hard. He was almost identical to Tad's bird, weighing fifteen pounds and having a six-inch beard. It was now mid-afternoon. The gobbler that I killed had gobbled on and off for about five hours. That was the only time, before or since, I've ever seen anything like that.

Turkey Dog Tales

A couple of days later, Rob and I took Jenny out to see if we could get Rob a bird. We arrived at our spot on Castile Run early that morning. I would generally wait at least an hour after daybreak before turning Jenny loose. I wanted to give the turkeys time to move around on the ground, which should provide more scent for Jenny to pick up. On this outing, our timing was perfect. We hadn't gone more than two hundred yards before Jenny picked up some scent. In short order, she had the gang scattered. A winded Jenny came back to us. Jenny and I set up with our backs against an oak tree. I had a large piece of camo cloth that I put on the ground for Jenny to lie on and then folded the top half of the cloth on top of her. This arrangement worked well to keep her hidden but also would allow her to quickly exit to go after a wounded bird if need be. I put Rob about twenty yards below our location.

After a short wait, we heard a bird calling in front of us. It answered as soon as I called. I figured it wouldn't be long before it showed up. This particular turkey decided to throw us a curve. It answered my every call, but refused to come any closer. I found out later that the turkey was across the main road, and that was the barrier that it refused to cross. It finally quit calling.

It had been about an hour since we had heard any calling. At just about the time we had decided to give up, we heard a bird calling over to our left. When I called back, it answered closer than before. Rob moved around the tree and got his gun up. The bird continued to get closer, but it turned and came in above us. Rob had to move further around the tree to get a shot. The turkey finally made his way down toward Rob. The bird came close enough that

Rob could get a good, clean shot. Rob fired, and the turkey, a nice young hen, dropped in its tracks. Our patience and persistence, two important traits to have when turkey hunting, had paid off for us on this hunt.

The season was still young, and Tad, Rob, and I had now each killed a bird. Tad and I decided we would go to a new spot that we hadn't previously hunted or scouted on Sweet Mountain. We would take both his truck and mine, parking one where we went in and the other where we intended to come out. This hunt would take us about three hours to complete. We used to hunt this area several years ago but hadn't hunted it since part of it had been logged. We were eager to see what we would find.

For the first part of our hunt, Tad and I hadn't seen any sign of our quarry. As we started off down the mountain on our way back to the truck, we started seeing fresh scratching. We were almost in sight of the main road when Jenny found the gang of turkeys we had been following. It was a large flock, and Jenny made a good flush as the birds left in all directions. We both passed up wing shots, wanting to do some calling instead. It was about mid-afternoon, and both my sons, Bert and Ben, would be getting off from school soon. We decided to pick them up from school, go home, pick up their hunting stuff, and get back in time to call some before dark.

Once we got back to the flush site, Tad and Ben set up about fifty yards from where Bert and I were. The first bird we heard calling was behind us. It could see our location from where it was. But because the turkey couldn't see another bird, it was stubborn and wouldn't come down to where we were and soon stopped calling. We heard another bird answering my calls from our right. It sounded as though it was

Turkey Dog Tales

desperate to find a buddy. The bird came in so that Bert couldn't see it until it was right on top of him. Bert fired his single barrel .12-gauge at twelve steps. The bird never knew what hit it. Upon examining the bird, I found that it had a beard but wasn't a gobbler; it was a bearded hen. She had a thin eight-inch beard. The beard had a dog leg crook about halfway down, which is typical for bearded hens. Jenny had a good first week with five gangs flushed. She had four kills to her credit, and two of those birds had been big gobblers.

October 1999; 12-pound bearded hen, Gratten, Tad, Bert, and Ben

Gratten Hepler

Possessing a natural ability that none of my other dogs had, Jenny could wind turkeys even if she hadn't crossed their path. On several occasions, I had witnessed her as she would stop, throw her head up testing the wind, and then take off to flush turkeys. During the summer and early fall, I would take her and let her ride in the back of my pickup. We would head for the Sweet Road, driving slowly along with Jenny still riding in the back. I could watch her in the rearview mirrors on the truck. Often, if she winded turkeys, she would jump up on the side of the truck bed, and her tail would start wagging excitedly. I would continue to move slowly, watching her. She would then run to the back of the truck and look back toward the area where she had first picked up the scent. If I was too slow in stopping the truck and letting her out, she would get impatient and jump over the side. She would run back to the spot where she winded the birds and take off down the mountain, flushing the flock. Sometimes, the birds would be close, or they could be as far as a half-mile away. I would check the road for tracks or other signs indicating where they had crossed. Finding none strengthened my belief that she had winded the birds and wasn't just trailing them on the ground. She did this on a regular enough basis to prove to me that she could indeed wind the birds from long distances.

Generally, I had better luck calling in birds from a flock flushed late in the afternoon as opposed to any other time of the day. It would be late enough in the day that there wouldn't be enough time for the birds to try to regroup before roosting. This is especially true when dealing with young turkeys. After spending the night alone, most young turkeys are more than anxious to find another turkey the next morning. I have seen many examples of this during fall hunting over the years.

One such hunt took place in the fall of 2000. Late one Sunday afternoon, before the season came in, Tad and I scoured the woods for signs of turkeys. Jenny picked up some scent, and with tail wagging excitedly, she took off up the mountain. Tad and I stopped and watched the sky for signs of the birds. We saw several birds take wing and fly down the ridge we were on. I glanced at my watch and knew that the birds would never have time to get back together before dark. We saw only six or seven birds in the gang. Since you rarely see every bird in the flock when they flush, we both felt there were probably more birds in the gang than we'd been able to see.

The next morning Tad, Rob, and I were back, waiting for the turkeys to begin calling. It was a perfect morning as far as the weather was concerned with no wind, a clear sky, and very cold. We'd made our approach to our calling location from above this time. This way, we wouldn't spook any birds walking our way in using our flashlights as we suspected all the birds to be below our position. I had decided to leave Jenny at home to rest up after her hard hunt the previous day. As soon as daybreak came, we heard kee-kees coming from down the mountain below us. We starting calling and got an answer from several locations.

The birds sounded like they were anxious to rejoin their lost buddies. After they left the roost, we could tell they were coming quickly, calling with almost every step. Four birds showed up, walking in front of Tad and Rob, but out of range for either to take a shot. The birds kept coming toward my position. At about twenty-five yards, I picked out a jake and fired, killing him and scattering the other three birds that had been with him. We decided to let things settle down and try to call in another bird. Less than an hour had passed before I called in another jake that Rob killed. Hoping to get Tad a bird, we called for another hour and a half but were unable to get Tad a bird from this flock.

October 2000; two good-sized jakes, Gratten, and Rob

Later in the day, Tad would get his chance at a bird after Jenny flushed another gang close to the Tucker Flats. He called in and killed a hen with less than thirty minutes of daylight remaining. Tad used a turkey decoy that he had nicknamed Gurdie. The idea was for the bird to focus on the decoy and not see the hunter. I'd never seen a decoy used in the fall prior to this, but it seemed to work. There was only one problem; Jenny, mistaking the decoy for the real thing, attacked Gurdie when Tad shot. As we headed back toward the truck with Jenny, we discussed the good fortune we had, and how none of us would forget the events of that day.

October 2000; turkey killed with the aid of "Gurdie" the decoy Tad, and Gratten

Two days later, Valerie's cousin, Charlie Filer, Todd, and I decided we would make a hunt on Potts Mountain. Our plans were for Charlie and me to take Jenny and work our way up a long hollow that meandered for almost a mile up the mountain. Todd would work his way to the top of a ridge that paralleled the path we would take. We had walkie-talkies to communicate back and forth in case either of us saw any birds. Charlie and I had gone about two hundred yards when Jenny got into some birds further up the hollow above us. I saw one bird coming right to us and told Charlie to get ready. The bird veered to our left and lit in a tree about fifty yards from Charlie. The shot was a long one, but Charlie let drive with his .12-gauge, tumbling the bird from its perch in the tree. I got on the radio and told Todd to hurry down to our position.

While Todd was in route to us, I saw another bird fly and land in a tree about seventy-five yards away. Todd saw the bird as he was coming down the mountain toward our location. He found a rest for his gun on a nearby tree and prepared to take a shot with his .22 magnum at about fifty yards. When he shot, the bird sailed out of the tree across the hollow and hit the ground running. He had hit the bird but had only wounded it. Jenny came back to us, and we took her up to where the bird had hit the ground. She started tracking the bird through the thick brush and had gone less than fifty yards when she found the bird hiding under some thick laurel. When we got to her, she had a mouth full of feathers. Every hunter hates to wound an animal and not be able to find it. Jenny made Todd's day by finding his wounded bird.

Later that fall, my son, Ben, and I took Jenny out for a walk on Sunday afternoon in hope that we might jump some birds. Just before dusk, Jenny flushed a bunch of birds, sending them to roost a little sooner than they had planned. I brought Ben and Charlie back the next morning. After seeing how well a decoy had worked while hunting with Tad, I decided to bring my jake decoy just to see what would happen. We placed the decoy on an old road so that it would be easily seen by any turkey coming to our calling. A gobbler started the morning off with his raspy yelping, and I answered him back with some excited yelps of my own. We saw the bird coming out of the pine thicket he had roosted in. When the gobbler came out in the road, he stopped and looked curiously at the decoy. The bird started toward it then moved back into the woods.

Turkey Dog Tales

The turkey had been so busy eyeing the decoy that he hadn't seen Charlie. Charlie fired, killing the gobbler in his tracks. We wanted to stay and try to get Ben a bird, but he had to get back to go to school. Ben is a very unselfish person and was as happy for Charlie's success as he would have been if he had been the one who killed the gobbler. By the time the season ended, Jenny had eighteen flushes and six kills to her credit that year.

December 2000; 17-pound gobbler, Charlie, and Ben

Gratten Hepler

The fall season of 2001 started off early for me. The fall season in West Virginia comes in a week before Virginia's season. I had taken several days to scout several different spots located on national forest land on the West Virginia side of Potts Mountain. I found a couple of good-looking spots where I had seen some scratching. On opening day in West Virginia, Jenny and I started hunting several of the spots where I had seen the least amount of signs during my scouting, holding the best spots to hunt later in the morning. The first couple of hunts came up empty. I decided to hit the spots I'd been saving.

When Jenny and I took off up Potts Mountain on a small ridge covered with white oaks, I started seeing fresh sign. Thinking it wouldn't be long before Jenny found and flushed these birds, I tried to keep her in sight in front of me. I knew she'd found them when I heard birds clucking and putting loudly just ahead of me. The leaves were still on the trees, and this hindered me from seeing in which direction the birds had flown or how many there were. Jenny came back to me, and we went up to the spot where I thought they had flushed.

As I worked my way up the mountain, I came to a spot on the ridge that looked like an ideal spot to set up. The woods were fairly open even though the leaves were still on the trees. I decided to build a blind and started to gather tree limbs and large sticks to use in the assembly process. I carry a small folding saw to help me with this chore. I was able to get enough branches and sticks to build a blind on three sides of the large oak tree that I would be sitting in front of. I built the blind high enough to cover me sitting down. I arranged the sticks so that I had a clear, unobstructed shot through them. I had done this several times

Turkey Dog Tales

in the past and found that a blind helped to break up my outline. The blind would also help cover any movement, especially if I had to move my gun at the last second. Even though I had Jenny covered up with a camo cloth, the blind would be helpful in hiding any movement she might make. It only takes a few minutes to build a blind, and you generally have plenty of time. It usually is thirty minutes or more before the birds start calling.

After waiting in the blind for about forty-five minutes, I heard a bird calling softly below me. I answered back and soon saw a hen making her way up the ridge. She was about seventy-five yards out when I first saw her. I was glad I had taken the time to build the blind. I knew that Jenny heard the bird calling and walking in the leaves as her whole body shook with every call the turkey made. Much to her credit, Jenny never moved. I let the hen come closer as she had no idea we were there. When she got within thirty yards, she stopped and started stretching her neck out trying to locate her buddy. I lined up the bead on her upper neck and fired. Jenny and I took off toward the downed bird. Jenny grabbed the bird before I got there, and I knew it wasn't going anywhere. I had been very fortunate to be successful in an area that I was unfamiliar with, and my scouting earlier really paid off.

Gratten Hepler

October 2001; opening day turkey in West Virginia

On the Sunday before the Virginia season was to begin, Tad, Ben, and I made our normal preseason Sunday afternoon walk in search of turkeys. Around mid-afternoon, Jenny flushed a gang, sending them off in all directions. We felt like it was early enough that the birds would try to get back together before dark. We sat down and waited just in case the old hen started calling. If she started calling, I would take Jenny and run her off so that she wouldn't have a chance to regroup her flock. It was a good thing we decided to stay. It wasn't long before we heard her start yelping loudly on the next ridge over. I told Ben and Tad that I would take Jenny with me and flush her. Jenny had heard the old hen calling by the time we had gotten halfway to her. Jenny left in the direction of the calling, and it wasn't long before I saw the old hen fly when Jenny flushed her. With her job done, Jenny

Turkey Dog Tales

came back to me, and we headed back to where Tad and Ben were waiting to continue our vigil until dark.

After a short wait, Jenny suddenly jumped up, looked up the mountain, and charged up the ridge. She hadn't gone more than a hundred yards before she jumped another gang. Most of these turkeys flew to the ridge to our right where the old hen had been calling earlier. With very little time left before dark, I took Jenny and headed back to the ridge to make sure that they didn't try to regroup at the last minute. Ben and Tad stayed put at the original flush site. It remained quiet as darkness came. We all met back at the truck well after dark. We praised Jenny for her good work that afternoon. Knowing we had two gangs of turkeys split up, we looked forward to the next morning's hunt with great anticipation.

I don't think Ben slept much that night, and to tell the truth, I didn't either. Our plan the next morning was to approach our hunting area in the dark from above so we wouldn't spook any birds going in. We drove in on the Sweet Road, which was right above the area where the turkeys had been flushed. Tad would take the first flush site, while Ben and I would head to the ridge where the second flock Jenny scattered had flown. The birds near Tad started calling before it was light enough to see. It wasn't long before we heard Tad calling too. One bird made a beeline for him, and we heard him shoot once, which we took as a good sign.

The birds in front of us were doing a lot of calling now. I had put Ben about twenty yards ahead of me. When Ben was younger and first started to turkey hunt, I would sit Indian style and put him in my lap. This gave me control over him and the ability to teach him about safety while hunting. As he got older, I let him sit beside me, and he proved himself to be a very safety-minded hunter. He was now thirteen and had killed several birds, both in spring and fall seasons. I had no reservations about putting him by himself.

It sounded like several birds were coming up the ridge right to Ben. I toned down both the volume and the amount of my calling as they closed the distance. I could see Ben sighting down the gun, but his barrel kept moving from left to right and back. When he shot, we both jumped up and took off toward the downed bird. I was surprised to see seven or eight more birds taking flight. One flared back over my head, giving me a great wing shot, and instinctively, I shot, dropping the bird. Afterward, I asked Ben why his barrel kept moving back and forth. Ben said he had his hood up on his camo coat to keep warm, but it hindered him in his ability to hear which way the turkeys would come. He said he had to shoot quickly when the bird showed up at close range. When Ben and I met Tad back at the house, I found out that we'd all scored that morning. The hunt certainly exceeded our expectations. We'd seen or heard probably twenty birds that morning.

October 2001; opening day "triple" in Virginia, Tad, Gratten, and Ben

After hearing about our good fortune on opening day, Rob was more than ready to get out with Jenny the next day. The morning hunt proved to be uneventful. That afternoon, Tad, Rob, and I decided to hunt in Moore's Bottom, and once again, Jenny came through with flying colors. The gang she jumped appeared to be small as we saw only three or four turkeys when they flushed, but they appeared to have all gone in different directions. One of the birds started calling in short order. Tad and I did some double-team calling, trying to make the lone bird think that several birds were getting together. It worked as the bird was coming steadily to our position. When it approached to about thirty yards, Rob got a clear shot and fired, putting the bird down for the count. We had taken four turkeys in two days, but they'd been taken from two different areas and from three different gangs. We are always very careful not to over-hunt an area or a gang of turkeys.

The next adventure with Jenny would take place on Potts Mountain. In my preseason scouting, I'd found a good crop of white oak acorns in the area I wanted to hunt. Late one afternoon, Jenny and I headed for the mountain in what I hoped would be an eventful hunt. Jenny stopped from time to time at the edge of the ridge where she could hear turkeys either scratching in the dry, noisy leaves or soft calling as they fed. She used all of her senses of sight, smell, and hearing to help her locate turkeys. I noticed she had stopped and was listening intently. She suddenly broke, disappearing off the ridge and down into the hollow below. Seconds later, I heard loud putting, and I knew she'd found what she had been looking and listening for. The birds took their only option by flying down the hollow, trying to escape from Jenny. By the time Jenny came back to me, it was late afternoon, and I knew I wouldn't have to wait long before darkness arrived.

That night, I called Charlie and told him of Jenny's success. He said he would be at my house early the next morning. At daybreak the following morning, Charlie and I were in the same spot I'd been in a little more than twelve hours before. I brought the jake decoy because the woods were fairly open. I set the decoy out about twenty yards in front of where Charlie would be sitting. I had a perfect spot to watch the hunt unfold as I could see Charlie and the decoy below me. I gave a soft tree call and got an answer from the ridge on the other side of the hollow. Soon, other turkeys chimed in. When they flew down from the roost, they got together below us but continued their calling. I began calling aggressively with loud cutting to try to bring the whole gang our way. They started moving our way, and I caught a glimpse of movement down the side of the ridge. Soon, the whole gang was visible from my position. I could see that they were all jakes. The lead bird, seeing the decoy, stopped in his tracks. After giving the decoy the once-over, he must have thought it was one of his buddies because he led the whole gang toward it at a quick pace. When Charlie shot, the jake hit the ground. The rest of the group quickly departed on the wing. Charlie's smile told his reaction to the morning's hunt.

Shortly after that hunt, Charlie said he had a duck hunting buddy, Joe, who had never killed a turkey and wanted to give it a try. Charlie tried to explain to Joe how we intended to use Jenny and what would happen if we were lucky enough to find and flush a flock. We decided to take Charlie's boat to Lake Moomaw the next day in an area where we'd seen turkeys the year before. Charlie, Joe, and I all met at the lake early the next morning and took a short ride across the lake into Bath County. Right after leaving the boat, Jenny found and busted a flock feeding on autumn olives. I called in one bird that came in quietly. Jenny had been lying with me while I called. She had heard the bird walking in the dry leaves before I had and raised her head up in the direction of the bird's path. This alerted me to the bird's arrival even though it was coming in quietly without calling. Jenny had done this on several occasions, letting me know when a silent bird was coming in to my calling.

There had been no way to let Joe know we had company coming because I'd made a mistake in putting Joe too far ahead of me. Unfortunately, Joe didn't see or hear the bird as it approached. I told Joe after the bird left that we would move down the ridge and call again in a different spot. We set up again, but this time I put Joe closer to where I was sitting. After calling for a few minutes, I got a response from another bird, a jake, that yelped and half-gobbled. He came quickly to my calls, stopping about thirty yards away, and jumped up on a big log. He continued his yelping and gobbling on top of the log, hoping to get a look at his buddy before coming any further.

Unfortunately, I didn't bring my decoy as this would have been a perfect time to have had one. From Joe's location, he couldn't see the bird because of a downed tree obstructing his line of sight. Finally, after not being able to see his noisy buddy, the jake got suspicious and turned around and left. He continued calling as he departed. He had really put on a show for us.

While we lamented our bad luck, we heard another bird start calling. This time, a hen came to my calling within ten yards from where Joe was sitting. I was just a couple of yards behind Joe, yelling underneath my breath, "Shoot, shoot!" No shot came. The bird spotted something she didn't like, putted, and left as quickly as she had come. To say I was frustrated would have been an understatement. Joe said he couldn't get a clear shot. In Joe's defense, I think he was being over cautious about taking a bad shot and missing or wounding the bird. I told him not to sweat it, that the day wasn't over yet. As I said this, I was thinking to myself that we would never get another chance that day. We decided we would go somewhere else for the afternoon hunt.

It was nearly lunchtime, and we were all hungry after all the excitement that morning. We ate lunch and went back to hunt in Moore's Bottom. We started our hunt around mid-afternoon. Jenny left us, and I watched as she headed up the ridge to our left. Thinking she was on the trail of turkeys, I told Joe

Turkey Dog Tales

and Charlie to keep their eyes and ears open. After Jenny had been gone for a couple of minutes, I saw a big turkey set its wings and glide down the top of the ridge. Then two more followed. We decided to set up about halfway up the ridge because two of the birds had flown off to an adjacent ridge. We chose an old blow down to get behind and use as a blind. We didn't have to do much work as the big downed tree made a good blind by itself. After an hour had passed, I heard a gobbler yelping, and I immediately answered him. I glanced over at Joe, and he appeared to be ready with his gun up over the log. I saw the bird coming with his beard swinging back and forth, and my heart starting pounding even harder. If you ever get to the point that your heart doesn't pound when you see a big gobbler coming to your call, it is time to give up turkey hunting and find another hobby.

The turkey veered to our right and started up the ridge to get a better vantage point. Joe's shot surprised me as I didn't think the gobbler was close enough, but the bird went down for good. This was a beautiful bird with a full ten-inch beard and weighing twenty and a half pounds. This was a tremendous bird for any hunter, much less for someone who had never killed a turkey before. I couldn't believe what had taken place that day. We jokingly told Joe that we knew he had passed up all the other shots just waiting for the right one. We took pictures at my house in the dark. All three of us were pretty wiped out after all the events of that day. I knew Jenny was tired too since she had done all the hard work of finding and flushing the turkeys.

November 2001; 20-pound gobbler, Joe's first bird, Gratten, and Joe

The next week, I took Jenny to the Bear Wallow land on Castile Run. We hunted our way out an old logging road and didn't see any fresh signs. Jenny and I were on our way back when she jumped a gang of about ten birds. I knew it was a good flush when I saw birds dispersing in all directions. One bird lit in the top of a white pine about seventy-five yards away. Jenny and I sat down to make sure they didn't try to get back together before dark. I hadn't heard any birds call, and I could still see the bird sitting in the pine tree as I left.

Knowing that we had a good setup, I gave John a call. He told me he could hunt a couple of hours before work. He met me at my house early the next morning, and we made the twenty-minute ride over the mountain. I brought my decoy this time. We set up with John in front of me, and I placed the decoy about twenty yards up the road to his right where it was readily visible. The calling started right after daybreak.

After I had called for a while, it was clear that the birds were spooked and had no intentions of heading our way.

Suddenly, a bird began calling not fifty yards behind me. It had slipped in quietly and decided to make its presence known. I made a couple of soft yelps and purred on my slate call. I could hear the bird walking. I think it could see the decoy, which helped to bring the bird into gun range. John was able to get turned around and see the bird coming. He had an awkward position to shoot from, but he made a good shot and killed the bird instantly. After we picked up the bird and decoy and started to leave, we flushed the same bird I'd seen the night before still sitting in the same pine tree. It never moved during all the calling and didn't even flush when John shot.

November 2001; Thanksgiving dinner for John and his family

Turkey Dog Tales

This would be the last bird killed from Jenny that fall season. Jenny flushed several more gangs in December, and we called several birds in but passed up the shots. This had been Jenny's best year yet. She had flushed twenty-four gangs with eight kills to her credit for the year.

In the latter part of May of 2002, we had a very hard frost that pretty much killed both the hard and soft mast crop for the fall. The wild turkeys as well as the other forest wildlife would have a hard time getting through the late fall and winter months. This was the case in every area I scouted during late summer. The turkeys would have to feed on insects early in the fall and then scrounge for whatever they could find later on.

On the day before the season opened, Tad, Ben, and I took Jenny to see what we could find. We decided to split up but keep track of each other with our walkie-talkies. Late in the day, Ben and I took Jenny to a ridge that started in the edge of a field and led up the mountain. Our thinking was that the birds might have been in the fields feeding before they headed up on the ridge to roost. As we started up the ridge, Jenny went on ahead of us, searching for signs. She went out of sight for a second in the brush. Shortly thereafter, I thought I heard a turkey cluck a couple of times, but I didn't hear or see any birds. I told Ben that Jenny had probably flushed one or two birds on the other side of the ridge out of our sight. We knew our chances were slim to have any luck there the next morning. But since we hadn't seen anything else, we had nothing to lose.

The next morning, Ben and I were up early. Our plan was to get Ben out for a short hunt before he had to go to school. Tad had decided he would go later in the day. The weather forecast showed heavy rain on the way that morning. I told Ben that since it was not raining yet, we would give it a try. We had to wait longer than normal for daylight due to the overcast skies. When it was finally light enough, I tried calling a couple of times with no response. I told Ben, who was just a couple yards ahead of me, to do some calling on his slate call. He had been calling for about fifteen minutes when I saw him put his call down and get his gun up. I was far enough away from him that I couldn't see what was going on. Just a few seconds had passed when he fired. We both jumped up quickly to see a mature hen lying in the leaves. He said that when he heard something walking in the leaves, he put the call down and got his gun up. When he saw a turkey appear in front of his gun barrel, he lined up the bead on the head of the turkey and fired. I congratulated him on his first bird that he had called in himself and killed.

October 2002; Ben's fall turkey that he called and killed himself, Gratten, and Ben

Turkey Dog Tales

Putting the call down and getting his gun up at the right moment is a very hard thing to do for even the most experienced hunter. Ben had really done a great job. A lot of hunters would have waited to see what was coming to get their guns up, and it would have been too late. Soon after we took a few pictures, it started raining. It rained hard the rest of the day, that night, and most of the next morning.

The rain finally let up enough that Tad and I could take Jenny for a hunt on the Bear Wallow land on Castile Run. We had gone out an old road for about half a mile when Jenny winded some turkeys and took off up the mountain right on their trail. When she flushed them, we didn't see but two or three birds, but we felt like there were more than what we'd been able to see. Tad set up on a finger ridge, and I set up about a hundred yards away on another little ridge.

It wasn't long before we heard the turkeys begin calling. Suddenly, the skies opened up, and it started pouring rain. To make things worse, the fog moved in on us, obscuring our vision past about fifty yards. One bird finally came in behind me. I'd made a critical mistake by not taking the time to build a blind. When I turned to try to get a shot, the bird saw me, putted, and flew. We kept calling as another bird was coming in behind us. This time, I got turned around before the bird got there and was able to kill the drenched bird, a jake. Tad came over to get a look at my bird, and as soon as he sat down, another bird started calling. With it raining so hard, it was hard to tell the direction of the bird's calling. We finally realized that it too was behind us. I knew then why we had seen only a couple of birds flying down the mountain when they flushed. Most of them must have run uphill, trying to escape from Jenny. Tad got turned around just as the bird showed up, and he made good on a very difficult shot. His bird turned out to be a young hen. I hadn't been this wet and miserable since our hunt during the flood of 1985. Those turkeys were determined not to let a little monsoon keep them from trying to get back together.

The wet weather continued for the rest of the week. Finally, at the beginning of the second week, we got to return to the woods. George and I planned to hunt an area known as Kimberlin Flats on national forest land. I had seen birds there during the spring season but hadn't been back since that time. Without much mast I wasn't sure if we would find any birds there. We started our hunt up an old service road that would lead us into a big white oak flat. After walking for about a mile without any luck, we started back toward the truck. On the way back, Jenny flushed several birds that had evidently fed through that area since we first came in that way over an hour ago. George and I began looking for a suitable spot to set up and begin calling. We found a large white pine, and I sat on one side with George on the other. An hour had passed when out of the blue a nice gobbler showed up about eighty yards away. Jenny hadn't heard it coming because the leaves were damp from all the rain, and the turkey hadn't been calling as it returned to the flush site. He kept walking toward us, and then he suddenly stopped about sixty yards away, looking for one of his buddies. He must have seen something he didn't like because he putted several times, turned around, and left.

Even though we'd lost a chance at that bird, George and I weren't ready to give up. I began calling with gobbler yelps and clucks and continued calling about every ten minutes. Finally, I got an answer from

Turkey Dog Tales

two different birds. One was in front of me and the other in front of George. The bird in front of George was coming in very slowly. The one on my side, however, was coming in fast. I told George he needed to get on my side of the tree. He quickly scrambled around to my side just in time to get his gun up before the bird's head popped over a rise. He made a clean kill with his .20-gauge magnum at twenty yards. The gobbler had a seven-inch beard, but when we checked it in, it only weighed thirteen pounds on certified scales.

November 2002; 13-pound gobbler, George, and Gratten

Gratten Hepler

When I cleaned the bird, I checked its craw and found it was completely empty. Since this was only early November, the worst weather and hardest times still lay ahead for the turkeys and other wild game. George's bird was the last bird to be killed that season. Jenny ended the season with eight flushes and four kills. She only flushed one-third of the gangs she had flushed the year before. To make matters even worse, we had a very wet spring in 2003, which hurt our early hatch numbers. I believe some of the hens that re-nested later that spring had a better survival rate with their poults.

In the fall of 2003, we were hit again with a poor mast crop that was probably due to all the wet weather we had the previous spring. There were a very few acorns in a couple locations. The soft mast had done a little better, but by the first of December, it would be gone. We did, however, see several large gangs during our preseason scouting that had in excess of twenty birds in them. One of these gangs was hanging out behind my house near some old grown-up fields. I thought this gang was made up of several old hens and their young. For whatever reason, the turkeys had decided to form one large gang rather than three or four smaller ones. We had nasty weather on the day before the season came in, and it continued through the morning hours on opening day. When the rain finally let up later in the day, Tad, Rob, and I got out and went looking for the large gang behind my house. We decided we could cover more ground if we split up. Tad and Rob went to one area, and I took Jenny to another. I hadn't gone far when Jenny ran head on into the large gang on a small finger ridge that bordered my property. I could hear and see birds flying in all directions as Jenny ran up the ridge. I got

Turkey Dog Tales

on my radio and told Tad and Rob that Jenny had located and flushed some turkeys. I told them to meet me on the ridge where the birds had flushed.

On my way to the ridge, I kept watching the trees, looking for birds that might still be sitting there until things calmed down. Suddenly, I spotted a jake perched high on a limb in a big white oak tree. He was intent on watching Jenny underneath the tree. He hadn't seen me yet, and when I fired, he fell within a few yards of Jenny. She jumped in on top of him, pinning the flopping bird to the ground. I called Tad and Rob to bring them up to date and tell them I would stay put until dark, which was approaching fast. I heard no more calling, so I took Jenny and headed for home. After meeting back at the truck, I told Tad and Rob that the table was set for a promising morning hunt.

October 2003; jake killed from large gang flushed by Jenny

The next morning, Tad, Rob and I had trouble finding our way back to the spot where we wanted to be due to heavy fog that had moved in during the night. Even with flashlights, it was hard to see any landmarks to know where we were. We finally stumbled our way to our spot and got set up. The turkeys started calling all around us, but the fog had them fouled up too. They stayed in their roost trees longer than they normally would have had the fog not been there. We could hear turkeys kee-keeing, clucking, cutting, and yelping. They were really putting on a calling exhibition.

Finally, one bird came to our calling. It came in behind Rob and flew up in a tree right in front of him no more than twenty-five yards away. He quickly dispatched the bird, and it tumbled to the ground. The other turkeys didn't pay any attention to Rob's shot as they kept right on calling. It sounded like several of the young birds had regrouped with one of the old hens. I thought about heading for her and chasing her off, but there was still a lot of calling going on, so I decided to stay put.

Just when we thought no more birds would come our way, we heard several birds calling behind us. They sounded anxious and were definitely headed in our direction. As the three birds came into view, the lead bird saw something amiss and starting putting. It was within shooting distance, and before it could run, Tad took the shot, killing the bird. We couldn't have asked for a better end to a great hunt. We had heard more calling that morning than I could remember hearing for a long time.

Turkey hunting is an activity Ben loves very much, but he can only hunt on Saturday since he had school during the week. He told me that he was looking forward to being able to go on Saturday. I took Jenny

Turkey Dog Tales

out on Friday afternoon with the hope of scattering a flock we could hunt the next day. I went to an area that I had seen turkeys in during one of my scouting trips before the season came in. Late that afternoon, Jenny found a small gang of birds as they fed up a hollow going toward their roosting area. Watching as Jenny flushed them, I heard another group of birds fly up to roost just above me. Jenny came back to me, and I took her to where I had heard these birds. She made enough noise in the dry leaves to scare those birds off the roost, sending them flying down the mountain. Now we had two gangs scattered in the same area. It was getting dark, so I headed for home with the knowledge that we should be in for a good hunt the next day. When I told Ben about our good luck, he couldn't wait until morning.

The next morning, Ben jumped out of bed like he was on springs. I'd never seen him do that on a school morning! We found our way down through the woods in the dark and got set up. We didn't have long to wait as we heard birds start calling on either side of our position. Both Ben and I were calling as the birds were closing in on us from both sides. We weren't sure which ones would get there first. Two anxious birds from our left soon answered that question. The first one that showed up was a jake only seven steps from Ben. The jake saw something that spooked him, and he flushed like a grouse. I admired Ben for not taking that shot on the departing bird. I wasn't sure that I could have kept from shooting at that bird when I had been his age. The second bird was far enough behind that it didn't pay any attention to the first bird flushing. It came up the same path the first bird had. Ben was ready and waiting when the bird showed up and he killed it on the spot. This was Ben's fifteenth turkey killed in his fifteenth year. Most of his birds had been spring kills, but he had several fall birds including this one to his credit.

November 2003; Ben's 15th turkey at age 15

For months, Ben and I had been planning to take an out-of-state hunt with Jenny. This meant we would have to choose a state that allowed dogs in the fall. We had several choices but finally agreed that Kansas would be the place. We searched for several months before we finally decided on an area to hunt. This area was made up of all private land consisting of several big farms that our guide had leased for hunting. In talking with the guide, he said the area we would be hunting had both Eastern and hybrid birds. The hybrid birds are a combination of Eastern and Rio Grande turkeys. I chose the last week of December for our trip as Ben would be out of school on Christmas break. The trip took about fifteen hours' driving time, and Jenny made the trip with no problems.

Turkey Dog Tales

While we were there, we saw a lot of turkeys with Jenny flushing two gangs. We saw a lot more gangs, but they were all in or near huge fields. The wooded areas were small and usually located between fields. Both gangs that Jenny flushed were either in a field or ran into a field when they saw Jenny coming. When Jenny would chase them, they could see her coming from a long way and stayed together when they flushed. One of these flushes took place at the end of a big cornfield. Jenny ran the turkeys out of the cornfield they had been feeding in and into a corner of the field with a narrow strip of woods bordering on a creek. Ben and I could see the birds as some flew across the creek and some flew up in the trees on our side. As the birds watched Jenny below from their lofty perch, we were able to get within gun range of them. We could see a large gobbler sitting in a huge oak tree, but neither one of us could get a clear shot with his head and neck hidden behind a large limb. We tried to get into a better position, but the wary gobbler saw us and flew. All of the birds had, by then, flown across the creek onto private land that we couldn't hunt on. This was the closest we came to killing a turkey from Jenny on our Kansas trip. Both Ben and I were successful in killing a bird, but we had to use other tactics other than flushing the birds with Jenny and calling them back. It was a great trip even though we hadn't been able to use Jenny as much as we had planned.

As the season came to a close, I would have one more opportunity to hunt with Jenny. Right after New Year's, I got a call from an old friend, Greg Hedrick. He said his brother-in-law, Mitch Childers, who lived in North Carolina, had told him that North Carolina was planning a one-week winter hunt in the middle of January, and it would be legal to use a dog for this

Gratten Hepler

hunt. Greg had told Mitch about Jenny, and Mitch gave me a call to see if I would be interested in bringing Jenny down for a couple of days to hunt. This would be Mitch's first opportunity to hunt turkeys with a dog. There hadn't been any fall hunting in North Carolina for thirty years. The plan was to have this season open in only a couple of northern counties.

The hunt would take place on about two hundred sixty acres of private land in Caswell County, North Carolina. Mitch said he had killed turkeys there in the spring season but had never been turkey hunting in the fall. I met with Mitch on Tuesday, and we hunted that afternoon. We only saw three turkeys in a field, but we saw a lot of sign. Mitch told me that there was a bigger bunch using the property.

The next day, we covered every inch of the property but still found no birds. On Thursday, we hunted with a few other guys, and we all hunted hard again but still didn't find what we were looking for. The others had to leave after lunch, so Mitch and I were on our own. I managed to kill a hen that evening as it came in to a roost site we had staked out earlier. I told Mitch that if we were patient and kept going back to where we had seen all the sign, sooner or later we would run into those birds. Since our hunting was confined to the two-hundred-and-sixty-acre tract only, I knew that the birds might be on land owned by one of Mitch's neighbors where we couldn't hunt.

The next morning, we were back to hunt one last time. Jenny went out ahead of us in a big hurry as if she had winded some turkeys. Sure enough, Mitch and I heard the sounds of turkeys putting as Jenny sent the birds into a frenzy. We saw at least eight birds as they scattered in all directions. We walked over to where they had flushed and saw a large area scratched up underneath the large oak trees. I told Mitch we needed to build a blind that would be big enough to hide the two of us and Jenny. We wasted no time in gathering old sticks and branches, using them in our construction process.

Example of a rough blind used by hunter and dog when calling turkeys

When the blind was finished, Mitch, Jenny, and I climbed in, and I made sure Mitch had good shooting lanes on all sides. We waited for about forty-five minutes before we heard a bird fly down and call. I immediately answered back. I heard it call one more time before it got quiet for good. I was afraid it would come sneaking in quietly, but it never showed up. Several minutes had passed when Mitch told me he heard a couple of wing beats to his right. Once the bird was on the ground, it called, and I called back. Every time I called, I got a response in return, each time closer. I glanced over at Mitch to see if he was ready. I got a glimpse of the bird making its way to us and saw a nice beard on the turkey swinging back and forth. As long as it kept coming our way, I was not going to call anymore, giving away our position even though we were well hidden. I saw Mitch move his gun slightly to the right, and then his .12-gauge magnum roared, instantly knocking the bird off its feet. Jenny was up and running before we were. I knew he had a nice gobbler when he shot, but I had no idea how nice until I got up close.

The gobbler's spurs were very long and as sharp as a razor. I glanced at my watch and told Mitch that it had been an hour since the flush. We took pictures, including one with the bird hanging from a tree limb by his spurs. After taking some measurements, we found the bird had a nine-inch beard and one-and-a-half-inch spur on one leg and one-and-nine-sixteenths-inch spur on the other. Having never been hunted in the fall before may have accounted for the reason the old gobbler came back so quickly. I told Mitch our patience and persistence had paid off handsomely with this bird.

Turkey Dog Tales

January 2004; Mitch's "Limb Hanger" from North Carolina

At the end of this hunt in January 2004, Jenny was seven years old. This year's ending totals for Jenny were twelve flushes and five kills. Her lifetime hunting accomplishments to date included ninety-three flushes, thirty-two kills, and three wounded birds she caught. I hadn't kept records with my other dogs but wish now I had. It is good to be able to keep up with their progress year by year. I know for sure that none of my other dogs have had the number of flushes or kills that Jenny has had. Jenny is a fantastic dog and as close to an ideal turkey dog as I will probably ever have. I know that Jenny's seasons are numbered and other dogs will follow her. But there will never be another Jenny.

POSTSCRIPT

To say that I am a lucky man is a true understatement, for I consider myself a very blessed man. I am privileged to have a loving wife who gives me all the "turkey time" I want. Valerie never complained, even when I took vacation time to turkey hunt. I'm also very fortunate to have two fine teenage boys, Bert and Ben, who are my pride and joy.

I am certainly blessed to have lived my entire life on a four-hundred-acre farm that borders on the George Washington National Forest, which afforded me the opportunity to hunt right out of my back door. Also, now that I am retired and can be my own boss here on the farm, I am able spend many wonderful hours in pursuit of turkeys. Having a good turkey dog by your side is the icing on the cake.

Since my dad took me on my first turkey hunt over forty years ago, I have been an avid turkey hunter. It's hard to imagine my life without being able to enjoy turkey hunting. Turkey hunting allows me fellowship with good friends during days spent surrounded by nature. It also gives me time spent with my turkey dog in the beautiful fall woods. To watch a dog working a flock of turkeys on a crisp autumn morning is as close to perfect as hunting can be. For the others who know the joy of using a turkey dog, no matter what the breed, they are already aware of what I am talking about.

It is my sincere hope you have enjoyed my *Turkey Dog Tales* and can see both the benefit and the joy a turkey dog can bring to your fall turkey hunting and your life.

ABOUT THE AUTHOR

Gratten Hepler is a 49 year old native of Alleghany County, Virginia. He still lives on his 400 acre farm where he was born, with his wife Valerie, and two teenage sons, Bert and Ben. He has been an avid turkey hunter for over 40 years and has trained and Fall turkey hunted with dogs for over 30 years. His successful hunting career has included hunting in 11 states other than his home state of Virginia.

Printed in the United States
23570LVS00002B/1-132